Obstacle Busting

How to get over, under, round and through every obstacle in your way

By Donna Higton

Also by Donna Higton

Fall in Love With Life
The First Step to a Joyful Life

ISBN 13: 978 1981272235
ISBN 10: 1981272232
www.donnaonthebeach.com
Edited by Aurora Dewater

Acknowledgements

Sincere thanks must go to my clients over the past decade or so – each and every one of you helped me to hone my obstacle busting skills and advice. I am so proud of all the obstacles you've busted over those years, and for proving that no obstacle is unbeatable.

I must thank my Creative Catalyst Circle on Facebook for giving me a space to talk about this book. We talked about the highs and the lows of writing, and you guys helped keep me writing this year. My community, who answered so many questions about what obstacles they were facing, and helped me decide what I needed to write, also deserve my gratitude.

As always, my friends and family are always there to kick my butt or show me love, depending on which I most need in the moment. Never underestimate how important every text, Facebook comment, conversation and random gif is in keeping me in my chair and writing.

And lastly, I want to thank every obstacle that put itself in my way. At the time, I didn't appreciate any of them. But now, I get it. Those obstacles have made me stronger, more resilient, and more able to reach for bigger and bigger goals. They also gave me 50,000 words worth of material. A true gift.

Contents

Introduction

Introduction

Welcome to the Obstacle Busting book – how to get over, under, round and through any obstacle in your way. I'm Donna and I've been coaching clients to create the lives they love since 2004. I've also been following my own dreams since the year 2000, and one thing I know for sure is that everyone gets stuck. Everyone faces what I call obstacles: blockages, fears, things that get in the way of creating the life you want to live.

Sometimes we think we're alone in this, that it is just us that gets stuck because so few people talk about all the ways they got stuck on the way to the life they wanted. Sometimes we think we're not supposed to get what we want and that if we come across a block in our path it means we shouldn't go that way. Sometimes we just get stuck and go no further, giving up on our dreams.

However, everyone will face obstacles and every problem is solvable. Every obstacle is get-over-able. Every block can be overcome. Sometimes, simply knowing that you are not alone in facing those obstacles is enough to help you keep going and get past them. I know that when someone has shared they too have felt self-doubt, or experienced resistance, or feared being seen, or got impatient, it has helped me to pull my socks up and get on with finding a way over, under, round or through anything getting in my way.

This book was conceived as a bonus mini-ebook to go with the "Create a Life Worth Falling in Love With" e-course. But the mini-ebook (which I intended to be perhaps 20 pages long) took on a life of its own and is now 5 times the size I thought it would be. It's perhaps not so surprising, because there are so many things that trip us up, get in our way, and cause us to stumble, falter and fall on the way to making our dreams happen.

I hope that you find a few new tools and ideas in this book to help you navigate any problems you might come across when working towards the life you dream of. You'll find 4 of the best ways to get past any obstacle at all in the "Shortcuts For Dealing With Obstacles" chapter on page 15. Then I've put in a big list of common obstacles with advice for dealing specifically with each one.

It's not an exhaustive list of obstacles, but a lot of the advice transfers to other obstacles, so if whatever is getting in your way isn't listed find one that's vaguely similar. Or just read them all, because the more ideas you have in your arsenal to deal with things that might make you get stuck, the easier it is to bust any obstacles that might block your path.

Also, if you can't find your obstacle (or something similar), feel free to get in touch with me at www.donnaonthebeach.com to share what you're dealing with, and get some help getting past it. I'm sure you won't be the only one who has experienced this and I'll help you work out some ideas for getting you over, under, round or through your obstacle.

Ultimately, I want to reassure you that everyone who strived for greatness, everyone who achieved anything wonderful, everyone who has dared to live their best, most joyous life, has faced obstacles along their path. This is the hero's journey, the quest, the adventure. Obstacles do not mean "go no further", they mean "sort this out so you can keep going and growing and loving your life even more".

So let's crack on with delving into how to get over, under, round and through anything that's getting in your way so you can get on with living a life you love and making your dreams come true.

Introduction
To Obstacles

Introduction to Obstacles

Put very simply, obstacles are simply things – beliefs, thoughts, circumstances, predicaments – that get in the way of you creating a life you deeply love. Obstacles can get in the way of any goal – writing a book, starting a business, getting fit, finding a career you love, finding love, and even deepening spirituality. They can be called problems, issues, roadblocks, hurdles, bumps, blocks, snags, stumbling blocks, challenges, hurdles and hindrances. They're all obstacles.

Obstacles are good for you.

They look like they're there just to cause you trouble, but these problems, issues, roadblocks, obstacles all exist to HELP you. They come up so that they can be dealt with. Once they're dealt with, you can move on with less baggage, less mess and more spring in your step.

Big Dreams and amazing lives stretch us, they call the best from us, and they ask us to be AWESOME.

In order to have the life you wish to have, you need to eliminate self-doubt and low confidence; you need to develop problem-solving muscles; you need to become all that you are capable of becoming.

And that means growing pains. It means obstacles. It means blockages. It means that in order to have things we've never had, do things we've never done, or be the best of ourselves we can be; things will need to change, we will need to grow, and obstacles will need to be overcome.

And also, this is life.

Shit happens.

What matters isn't whether you fall down (you will) or get stuck (you will), but how you get up and keep going.

How you get over, under, round and through every obstacle in your way is what matters.

The trouble is, most of the time, we don't deal with what's getting in our way. For example, we don't know what to do so we do nothing, or we believe that people like us can't have what we want and we never challenge that belief, or we realise we have some fear, negativity or discouragement so we move away from the dream that's causing that uncomfortable feeling.

But imagine that you could figure out what to do and do it. You could change that belief to "YES I CAN" or just go ahead and try anyway despite the belief that people like you can't. You could notice the fear, negativity and discouragement and meet them head on. If you find a way to either completely deal with these issues, or just make them a little better, life will be easier from that point on. So from that perspective, the original problem helps to make your life better.

Your obstacle, blockage or problem can help you see that there is a better way.

For example; I had a lot of resistance to working on books and courses in my business. After attacking this obstacle a few different ways (mainly charging head on like a bull at a gate), I realised I was making it hard for myself to make time for those things. Instead of taking an hour here and there, I was insisting on taking days at a time, and free days were difficult to find, so I ended up doing nothing.

Eventually I figured out that I could make it easy for myself, I could do the best with what I had, and I could chill out about wanting it all done yesterday and just take my time working through what needed to be done. 25 minutes here, an hour there, until I found a routine that worked for me.

Obstacles are not put in your path to piss you off (although sometimes it feels that way).

They are there so you can move past them, through them, over them, or under them.

Think of obstacles as resistance or strength training for your life navigation muscles. They are there to tell you that life can be better and if you fix this issue, it will be.

So what issues, problems and obstacles come up for you time and again?

Can you imagine if that problem was solved, once and for all?

How much better would your life be if that issue no longer existed?

Take your problems, issues, niggles, upsets, roadblocks and challenges as your cues that something can be changed.

Even if you're convinced there's nothing you can do…there is usually something. It may only be a small thing, it may not fully solve the problem, it may *just* be a change in attitude (which can often lead to the biggest transformations), but there is usually *something* you can do.

1% progress is still progress

Doing something to make a problem just 1% better counts as progress. You can't always fully delete every issue immediately: you might need to chip away at it a bit first. If you can make a 1% change today, and another 1% change tomorrow, and so on – in a little over 3 months, the problem will be 100% better. Isn't that preferable to doing nothing at all and staying stuck?

Take some action to change things. Play the long game – especially with big problems that have been around for years. If it's going to take a year to sort it, start now and take that year to sort it. If you don't know what to do to fix it, find out. Ask for help, search the internet, or get a coach.

Welcome obstacles as the catalysts for positive change they are. Once you sort them out, life will be as you've always known it can be – easy, effortless and fun. With the odd problem, challenge and obstacle thrown in to show you that it can always be even better.

Obstacles are the same for everybody

When you have been obstacle-busting for a while, you start to notice something – everyone faces obstacles, and the obstacles are often the same for everybody. Whenever I speak to clients about the obstacles they're coming up against, they think it's just them that's having trouble. They think that they are deficient or defective or doing it wrong. Not so. Anyone who does anything that expands their world, like following a Big Dream, will find their path peppered with hurdles.

The first time I worked on a creative project, I came up against the following obstacles: never getting started, resistance, life got in the way, self-doubt, fear, wondering who was I to do this, problems finishing the project...and more. Everyone I know who has created anything has come up against at least some of the same issues. People I don't know, whose blogs or biographies I've read, come up against at least some of the same issues.

Everyone comes up against obstacles – it's not a deficiency in you. I guarantee that someone you admire who has done what you want to do has hit obstacles and overcome them. But many people don't discuss their dark times and problems. They present a happy, competent, confident face to the world, even if behind the scenes they're sad, in utter chaos and riddled with self-doubt.

Many famous authors, actors and musicians have shared their problems with self-doubt, with stage-fright, with thinking they would never make it. Listen to these stories and hear not only that they got past their obstacles, but also that they HAD them in the first place. They're just like you. It is simply part of the journey to bump up against obstacles in your path.

People who are loving life are not people who never have any problems – we all have problems in our lives – but they're the people who are confident they can overcome whatever life puts in their path. They're the people with strong obstacle-busting muscles.

It's not me, it's them

By the way, don't go giving your power away by saying "if THEY would change, this would be better". It may well be true, but unless you intend to hold them at gunpoint to *make* them do as you say (not a strategy I recommend), it's out of your control. **Focus on what YOU can do to make changes in YOUR life.**

When you take full responsibility for your own life, and refuse to blame anyone else or give anyone else the reins of your life, life is in your hands. If it's down to someone else to make you happy, it's totally out of your control. So even if there is someone causing trouble in your life, or doing their best to upset the apple cart, take back your power.

Decide it's your life, and there are still decisions you can make and actions you can take to improve your life, no matter what other people are doing. If you're waiting for the rest of the world to fit perfectly into your perception of how life should be so you can be happy…you're going to be waiting a long time. Ironically, when you decide to do your best to make your life and yourself the best you can be, the outside world often falls into line.

But even if it doesn't you're still working on your own life, and doing the best you can with the circumstances and relationships you have.

Obstacles are signs of growth

It is normal to hit obstacles – everyone faces them at some point (or at several points). It's normal to hit walls as you grow and go for what you want. They are nothing to be afraid of. Don't let them stop you, they're there to strengthen you, to build your creative muscles, and to make you the best you can be. Although they are infuriating, try as much as possible to relax and just tackle each obstacle as you come across it – no drama, no stress, and no worries.

Most obstacles look more scary and unassailable than they actually are.

Start trying to get over, under, round and through the obstacles and a way will be found. I guarantee it. But if you feel seriously stuck, and nothing in this book helps you to overcome your obstacle, then get help – from friends, from the Divine, from coaches, mentors, teachers, anyone you can find who might be able to assist you. You don't have to do this alone.

It is a myth that getting the life you want should be easy.

This myth can be one of the biggest obstacles of all. Yes, there is a beautiful flow to going after the life you want, a sense of rightness. It also asks a lot of you, challenges you, makes you confront anything that could get in your way – and that doesn't feel easy at times. That doesn't mean you should give up (unless you don't want what you're going for, in which case find something you truly want and go for that). It just means you have an obstacle to deal with. When you deal with that obstacle, life will be better and the path will be easier.

Sometimes it takes a while for you to see the difference, but trust me, each obstacle you overcome will make the path smoother. Each time you navigate and overcome and get past an obstacle, you get stronger; and the next time it, or something similar, comes up, you know what works (and perhaps what doesn't).

Eventually you will start breezing past these challenges, barely pausing to notice them. This is what I believe happens when people say they don't have any challenges. They do, they just barely notice them anymore because they're so good at getting over any obstacle in their way.

Obstacles may be a sign saying 'don't go that way'.

Sometimes you don't get what you want because it's not the right thing for you; it's not the right direction for you. This is what people mean when they say that following a dream should be easy because life will turn you away if it's not the right path. There's a big difference between a sign saying 'don't go that way' and a sign of growth. Your inner wisdom will tell you if an obstacle is there for you to overcome, or if it is pointing you in a different direction.

Although following Big Dreams can be deeply challenging, this does not mean you need to bang your head against a brick wall. Because I am stubborn (tenacious), I will tend to stay with things that aren't working for a little longer than I should sometimes. If you have the same tendencies, learn to check in with your inner guidance to see if you are being tenacious, persistent and determined or obstinate, pig-headed and unreasonable. If it's the latter, there may be a better path for you. Just a thought.

You may fall into the opposite camp where at the first sign of trouble, you run. I understand that impulse. I often want to give up, but there's a voice within that tells me to keep trying. If you have a tendency to drop your dreams like hot cakes as soon as an obstacle raises its ugly head, just try a bit of obstacle busting and stick with your dreams a little longer.

My litmus test for this is: have I tried everything I can think of and do I still want this dream? If I haven't and I do, I'm not done yet. Sometimes it feels like following a Big Dream is just one big obstacle course, but that's OK. Just think of the increased level of confidence you'll have, the creative muscles you're exercising, the Superhero Obstacle Busting Skills you're developing. Your inner wisdom will tell you when the obstacles are telling you to change direction.

Little obstacles can stop you just as effectively as big obstacles.

How stuck you get because of an obstacle is no indication of how big that obstacle is. I've lost count of the number of conversations I've had with clients where they've been stuck for a long time because of a particular obstacle but the solution is super quick and easy. Imagine walking through the woods and getting caught on a thorn, and struggling to get free (ever done that?). You can stay stuck in that thorn bush for a while.

But if you stop and examine why you're stuck, instead of struggling to get free and getting yourself more firmly caught in the thorns, you can see it's just a thorn, unhook yourself and away you go. Often the obstacle, once we stop and look at it, is not as monstrous as we first fear – the monster under the bed is often just a sock. If you don't look at the obstacle, you will never know if it is a huge scary monster or just a sock.

So don't think that if you've been stuck for a while, this means your obstacle is a big monstrous issue that will take 1000 years to deal with. It might be quite simple – like the client who kept beating herself up for not having done anything yet with her fledgling business. She simply took one action a day for a month and that thorn in her side was gone.

Sometimes all you need is a suggestion of a solution to get you moving. Some obstacles are more troublesome of course, but that's ok – they will build your obstacle-busting muscles up even more.

Multiple obstacles

When I was in the final edits of this book, I asked my community to share some of the obstacles that were stopping them from having the life they wanted. Almost everyone who shared had multiple obstacles. It wasn't just one thing stopping them, it was 2-6 different things getting in the way. So don't be discouraged if you recognise every single obstacle I talk about in this book – that's just life.

We all come up against fear, self-doubt, life getting in the way, no money, realism, cynicism, discouragement, self-sabotage. Sometimes all at once. One obstacle can act as a magnet, drawing other obstacles to you. Like when you have self-doubt, so you don't get started or don't get finished, and then self-criticism kicks in, followed closely by cynicism and negativity and because all this is going on, you find yourself resisting doing anything (unsurprisingly).

It really doesn't matter how many obstacles come up. All the obstacles can be overcome. OK, tackling one is easier than tackling 15, but often once you start working on one obstacle the others lose their power over you too. If you manage to find the original, magnetic obstacle drawing in all the others, it may be the only one you need to vanquish for all the others to simply disappear.

But even if you don't, getting rid of anything in your way makes you stronger and more capable and works your obstacle busting muscles, making it easier to get rid of other things getting in your way. It's worth bearing in mind too that you do not need to completely obliterate an obstacle. If you think of it as something blocking the path you're walking, you only need to be able to navigate around or scramble over it to keep going on your path.

We sometimes think we need to be perfect to go after our dreams; perfectly confident, perfectly skilled, and perfectly turned out with great hair. The truth is that we just need to be able to move forward – sometimes with just a shred of confidence, a little bit of skill and looking like we were dragged through a hedge backwards. Believe me, the people who've done whatever you want to do never had all their shit together either.

Boomerang obstacles

The boomerang obstacle is one that just keeps coming back. You think you've licked your fear of failure, or your self-doubt, or your energy and health issues but here they are again. It doesn't mean you failed to get rid of it, it just means that some obstacles are like dust. No sooner have you dusted and polished than another speck of dust appears, and before you know it, it looks like you haven't dusted in a century.

It's the nature of obstacles and blockages to re-appear.

Sometimes you just do what you did last time and move on past; sometimes you need to dig deeper this time and find other ways around, under, over or through the obstacle. Sometimes you find the 3-headed monster has grown another head to deal with, like a hydra – another aspect of the same obstacle, and eventually you will just recognise it as the same thing again and carry on regardless.

I mentioned earlier some of the obstacles I came up against when I first started working on creative projects. That was over a decade ago and I still hit many of those obstacles when working on new books or projects now. They're much easier to deal with now though. Obstacles that 10 years ago would have me crying or running away to hide barely cause me to break stride any more.

I mostly just ignore them. Or give the fears 10 minutes of my time, and then carry on with what I was doing. Some still have the power to make me stumble or stress me out, but then I just figure out a way over, under, round or through.

If things you've dealt with before come up again, deal with them again and keep moving.

I know it doesn't feel that simple in the moment when you get stuck, but really, it is. Eventually you'll have such strong obstacle busting muscles that no obstacle can get in your way, no matter how many times it comes up or how many disguises it wears.

Obstacles versus excuses

Don't worry, I'm not here to bust your chops and give you grief about the excuses you're making. I just want you to recognise the difference between an excuse and a genuine obstacle that you need to deal with. We've all done it "oh, I can't do so and so because I don't have time/money/confidence/another excuse"…and the excuse is bullshit.

You can just treat your excuses as obstacles and use all the tools in your toolkit to get over, under, round and through them, but there might be a shortcut. Ask yourself:

What if this was an excuse, why would I be stopping myself from moving forward?

Sometimes when you ask that question, you find there's a real obstacle hiding behind the excuse. For example, one of my clients was using the excuse, "I don't have time". When asked "what if this is an excuse, why would you be stopping yourself from moving forward?" She replied, "I'm scared". Fear was the real obstacle, hiding behind a mask of no time. Once she'd dealt with the real obstacle, she suddenly found the time.

You also may find that you're making excuses because you don't want whatever it is you're going for. One of my clients wanted to start a blog, but kept making excuses. When they investigated why, they realised they didn't really want to do it! They'd been told by a marketing expert that they had to have a blog to be taken seriously, but the idea of sitting down every day to write a blog post felt like a huge, boring chore. So they ditched the idea, and decided to take on leadership roles to establish their authority.

Aside: whenever anyone tells you that you have to *do something, unless they're trying to save your life, check in with your inner guidance. If you don't want to do it or you don't agree with it, it'll be a painful process to try to force yourself to do it…if you ever do. Your resources would be better spent elsewhere.*

Other times, you'll find that you're making excuses because you think it's going to be hard work, because you haven't taken the time to see clearly what to do next, out of habit, or even for no apparent reason. Sometimes just questioning what's going on will make the excuses disappear in a puff of smoke.

Getting past your obstacles

In each section of this book, there are suggestions for actions to help you get past your obstacles. Do not take these actions to be the *only* things you can do – also think for yourself, what could you do? You are intuitive, wise and creative. I can see that about you from here. So don't just rely on my ideas, also think of your own actions to take to get past anything that is blocking you.

Keep in mind that there IS a way past or through every obstacle and that you can find that way.

If those two things are true, nothing can ever stop you from getting what you want.

Obstacles aren't real

At the core, none of this stuff is real. It's what we make up, what we use to rationalise why we're stuck, what we create to make life difficult for ourselves.

So you may wonder why I'm writing a book about something that isn't real...

Because it feels real.

When I told one of my clients that these obstacles and challenges and blockages and fears were not real, that she'd made them up, it totally freed her from them. Whenever she felt stuck, she'd say "this is not real, I'm making up that I'm stuck" and she'd carry on, moving forward with confidence and power.

Another client I had the exact same conversation with replied with some asperity "well, they feel very real to me". Most of the obstacles I've met along the road felt pretty real to me too. It took me many years to get to the point that the idea they're not real was at all freeing for me.

So this book is for those of us stuck in the illusion. If we can find our way out, over and over again, we'll start to see that these obstacles aren't real. In the meantime, we've got our version of Ariadne's string to get us out of the maze.

Shortcuts for dealing with obstacles

While it can be useful and sometimes it's necessary to deal with the specific obstacles that are coming up and getting in your way, sometimes there is an easier way to get past the obstacle. Particularly once you're experienced in dodging past and busting through your obstacles, simple things will help you to get unstuck. Here are four things you can try before you put your cape and obstacle-fighting pants on:

1. Take action

If you ever feel stuck, try this first:

Identify the next step. Break it down into a baby step and do it. Repeat.

It's really that simple. Take some action. Identify what's next – what do you need to do next? (And if you don't know, your next step is to figure out what's next.) Then break that action down into a baby step. A baby step is an action that can be taken in 10-

15 minutes. Most people have a tendency to pick next steps that are huge projects – like writing a book or creating a website, and this can be utterly paralysing. So break it down into a teeny, tiny, easy-to-take baby step and crack on.

One of two things will happen. Either you will stop being stuck, because you've created a bit of momentum and you're moving, or you will hit an obstacle. Both are good. The first means there is no problem. The second means you have a better chance of identifying and eliminating the obstacle because you're running smack-bang into it, not avoiding it by not taking action.

2. Check your foundations

If your foundations are rocky, life is more difficult. When we don't take care of ourselves, give ourselves love, honour our energy, enjoy life and get support, obstacles can more easily catch up with us and take us down. Who has the time to take care of these foundations – we're all so busy and stressed.

The irony is that if you take the time to build strong foundations, you will be able to do so much more with your wonderful life. If you don't, you'll only get so far before it all comes crashing down. Most of us act as if we're superwoman – we go and go and go and go and do, do, do…until we are exhausted, depleted and wondering if this is all there is to life.

(It's not.)

So take care of your foundations.

Self-care

You need to take excellent care of yourself – the better you feel, the more you can do, the more you can give, the more you will enjoy your life (and isn't that the point?). So check in with your self-care – are you feeling cared for right now?

Take a moment to breathe into your heart and ask: How cared for am I feeling right now on a scale of 1-10, where one is *not at all cared for* and 10 is *cradled in the arms of love*. If it is less than a 7, your only task is to do something to make yourself feel more cared for by doing something that nourishes you.

Body, mind, heart and soul

You have *all* these aspects of yourself and they *all* need great care. Most of us take care of our physical body - if we take any care of ourselves at all - but you also need to be taking care of your mental health, your emotional health and your spiritual health. Check in with your body, mind, heart and soul to see how you're feeling in each area and what each part of you needs.

For more on this check out this article: http://www.donnaonthebeach.com/blog/wisdom, and the Body, mind heart and soul Guidance Recordings at http://www.donnaonthebeach.com/blog/guidance.

Self-love

You deserve your support, your backing. You deserve to believe in yourself 100%. You deserve your love and approval. You deserve your encouragement and faith in yourself. Imagine what it would be like to be fully loved and supported by another person and give that to yourself.

Take a moment to breathe into your heart and ask: How loved do I feel right now (by myself) on a scale of 1-10, where 1 is *I don't feel at all loved* and 10 is *I back and support myself 100%.* If it's less than a seven, your only task is to do something loving for yourself. Be kind to yourself, be encouraging, and give yourself the time and space to do something loving for you.

Energy

How's your energy right now? Could you lay face down on the floor and stay there quite happily? Or are you energised and full of life? You need re-fuelling, especially when you are very busy and important (and I know you are!) so make sure you are taking care of your energy.

Take a moment to breathe into your heart and ask: How energised am I feeling right now on a scale of 1-10, where one is *I have no energy* and 10 is *I feel like Tigger, bouncy, bouncy, bouncy!* If it is less than a 7, your only task is to do something to raise your energy – do something fun, get out in nature, do something you love that energises you.

Joy

What's the point of life if not to enjoy it to the fullest? It's so easy to get stuck in a rut and get stressed and joyless, but don't let that happen to you – joyous energy is so strong, it makes life a breeze.

Take a moment to breathe into your heart and ask: How much am I enjoying life right now a scale of 1-10, where one is *I'm not enjoying life* and 10 is *I am totally in love with my life.* If it is less than a 7, your only task is to do something fun, something you enjoy because this is your life. ENJOY it.

Support

No man is an island, or so they say, but genuinely we don't have to do everything ourselves. We can get help and support from those around us. In fact, people LOVE to help, so stop trying to be superwoman and get the support you need. Ask for what you need whether it's encouragement, practical support, empowerment, cheerleading, love, hugs, chocolate, a sympathetic ear, or a sounding board. You probably know people who are natural cheerleaders or chocolate buddies – spend time with them and get the support you need.

When all these foundations are strong, fears melt away, obstacles look smaller and sometimes they disappear entirely – so make sure you are taking great care of your foundations.

3. Check in with your guidance

I cannot tell you how many obstacles have been overcome by simply taking a little quiet time, letting my thoughts pipe down and letting guidance come through (whether inner guidance or higher guidance). Usually in under 10 minutes an answer is provided that helps me get unstuck. These days, we are bombarded with so much information – social media, Auntie Google, 2000 TV channels. It is rare that we take the time to go in (or up) for guidance.

But it is the most reliable guidance system you have – your inner wisdom (and higher wisdom) knows so much. You know so much more than you give yourself credit for. Often, I will ask clients what they need to get past an obstacle and they will say "I don't know" without giving it more than 2 seconds thought. When they are allowed (some might say *forced*) to sit with the question for a couple of minutes, an inner answer ALWAYS comes.

Your body, mind, heart, soul, intuition, higher self and any divine beings you believe in are always there for you, with wisdom to share. Many of us trust outside sources more than ourselves – we look outside for answers and magic pills. But the truest answers and biggest magic are within you. So do what you do to connect with that guidance. If you need help with that: for inner guidance, check out my Body, Mind, Heart and Soul Guidance program:

http://www.donnaonthebeach.com/blog/guidance. And for higher guidance, make sure you're on my list at www.donnaonthebeach.com because there's a book on higher guidance percolating.

Think of an obstacle you are facing at the moment, and just get quiet. Go sit outside for 5 minutes, or in a room away from distractions and just let your mind roam. Don't try to think of a solution, just be still. You can focus on your breathing if that helps you, you can dance to a song you love if that helps you, you can work with a mantra or guided meditation, you can watch the clouds or trees or stars or waves (online if you can't do this in real life).

However you do it, be still and let your inner (or higher) wisdom speak to you. What do you know deep in your heart and soul that you need to do about this obstacle?

And if you hear "I don't know", keep listening, that's just the first answer out of the pipe. Stick with it and let more answers come. Too often we stop at "I don't know", not realising this is not guidance or truth, but a kind of knee-jerk thought. After that knee-jerk thought will come another answer. Stay calm, keep breathing and keep allowing space for answers to come. They will.

Of course, practice makes improvement with hearing your guidance. If you're not used to listening to your inner or higher guidance, you may need to give yourself more time or to play with how you best hear your guidance. Here are a few ideas that have worked for me and my clients:

• Dance - get into your body and out of your head and answers can magically appear. Or at worst, you've had fun dancing!

• Do yoga – again focusing on the body clears the mind.

• Run – the same happens.

• Take to the page – get a pen and paper and ask for guidance and write down whatever comes through. One of my clients did this and after half a page of "this is stupid" and "Donna's wrong, no answers are coming", alakazam! The answer came.

• Sit and watch the sun rise or set, or the stars or the trees, or the waves or the clouds, and let your mind roam until an answer arrives.

• Talk to yourself – it's not a sign of madness, it's a sign of genius. Often, the words help release answers.

- Create – draw/paint/make something – this keeps a part of your mind busy and allows the still, small voice within to be heard.

Learning to hear and trust your inner and higher guidance is one of the most impactful things you can do in life. When you can hear and trust the wisdom that is given to you, you have a way past every obstacle that might get in your way.

4. Become a ninja problem-solver

Now, this 4th suggestion is more of a long-term strategy than a quick fix. We are all infinitely creative and wise, but when we forget that, we let our problem-solving muscles become flabby with underuse. Those muscles are still there – strengthen them. Don't believe me that you are infinitely creative? Look back at all the excuses you've made up NOT to do something. I rest my case.

I've lost count of the number of times I've heard from clients "I've tried *everything*" when they've actually tried 2 or 3 things (or…my personal favourite, a client who'd tried ONE thing and said to me "I've tried *everything*"). I'm more of a plan A-Z kind of person. Not that I want to get to Plan Z, but I'm endlessly stubborn, so there's no way I'll stop at Plan A, B or C.

Have you heard the story about Thomas Edison and the lightbulb? He tried 1000 different ways to get it working before it finally did. That's the story of pretty much every invention known to man. Had he given up at 2 or 3 attempts and said "I've tried *everything*", we might still be reading by candlelight.

So exercise those creative muscles and try. Attack all challenges from every angle. Become a ninja problem-solver – but remember to make it fun!

Do not make it boring (steering committee meetings, anyone? YAWN).

Do not make it stressful.

Do not tie your self-esteem to how quickly you can do it.

Do not try to soldier on alone if you're struggling.

Do not frown and sweat.

Let it be fun.

Let it be easy.

Approach it with a light heart and a curious mind.

Ask "how could I…" instead of "why can't I…"

Ask "what can I do" instead of saying "I can't do X".

Ask "what if" instead of saying "it's impossible".

Ask others instead of isolating yourself (because ninja problem solvers know that other people are an amazing resource).

When you don't know what to do…figure it out.

Smile and play – good ideas come from good feelings.

An obstacle is a puzzle for you to solve, and even if you don't love to solve a puzzle, you may as well try to enjoy it because life's going to throw you a few knots to unravel!

Ninja problem solvers also know when to back off and go have fun – sometimes an obstacle will be overcome with some distance, rather than hours of trying and bashing your head against a wall. Thanks to my stubborn nature, I often try and try and try with no success, and then the moment I give up, the light-bulb comes on and I figure it out.

"When you have exhausted all possibilities, remember this – you haven't." Thomas Edison

Computer games are great examples of how to get past an obstacle.

In the vast array of Facebook games available these days, there is a wonderful lesson for how to get past obstacles:

- Keep trying.

- Attack it from all directions.

- Occasionally swear and mutter and chunter and abandon the game altogether, but then go back and try again, and again.

- If you've been stuck a while, get help. Auntie Google has lots of help available.

Apply the same determination and detachment to your obstacles – you're going to get past them. Somehow.

And if none of these things – action, strengthening foundation, inner wisdom or ninja-ness - gets you past your obstacles, there are 44 obstacles detailed ahead with lots of ideas for how to get over, under, round and through whatever's getting in your way.

Warnings

Don't get so distracted by dragon slaying that you forget your treasure!

Obstacle-busting can be fun, it can feel like a win, and it can be compulsive. I wrote this book so you'd have a resource to help you when you hit obstacles, not to help you avoid your dreams because you're so busy obstacle-busting! See obstacle busting as dragon-slaying. You need to slay any dragons that cross your path; but you don't need to go looking for dragons to slay!

The obstacles will come up on their own as you move forward, and the more you go for your dreams, the more obstacles you'll come across. You won't need to go in with your sword swinging every time. You'll learn which dragons you can sidestep, which are friendly dragons pointing you in a new direction, and which you will need to slay to move on.

But the only reason to slay your dragons is so you can get to your treasure. It's easy to get distracted and think you need to fix every single obstacle I mention. You don't. You could…but honestly I suspect it would be a distraction. Keep your eyes on your treasure – keep your focus on what you want to create in your life. Let Obstacle Busting give you the tools (sword, shield, dragon-language to befriend dragons) but only use them when necessary.

The more you focus on what's wrong with you, the more you will find to fix.

You don't need fixing.

You simply need to know that sometimes obstacles come up that get in your way and your job is to get past them, and get on with going for the life you want.

Don't try and take it all in at once.

There's a lot of information in this book. If we were coaching together, I wouldn't dream of throwing it all at you in one sitting like this, it would be far too overwhelming. So if you read the whole book, do it as an overview of the subject, not to try to take everything in immediately. Trust yourself to pick up what you most need right now, and know that the book will still be here when you next hit an obstacle and need a reminder of how to get over, under, round or through it.

Specific Obstacles

Specific Obstacles

The following sections contain the most common obstacles I've come across in the past 15 years of both coaching and Big Dream following. It's not a totally exhaustive list, so if you can't find your particular obstacle, look for one that is similar and see if any of the ideas will work in your situation, or simply read them all. There's a lot of crossover in obstacle busting, so have a look at the solutions and see if any of them might work for you.

The first obstacle (below) is a standalone, but I've grouped the other obstacles together to make them easier to find, and to make this section easier to read. May you easily get over, under, round and through every obstacle in your path.

'Yeah, but' and 'my situation is different'

Before we get into the other obstacles, I just want to tackle this one. Often, when I talk to clients about getting past their obstacles, they resist the answers. Because their situation is different, there's a 'yeah, but...' Like, "I know everyone you've ever spoken to about this has found some time, but *I* won't because *my* situation is different." Like, "I know you say self-care will help, but I can come up with 12,000 reasons that I can't or it won't."

When coaching clients, I usually listen patiently then say, "Give it a try and if it doesn't work, you can tell me I'm wrong then". 90% of the time whatever I'm suggesting helps and the other 10% of the time, with a small tweak, it helps. These things do work *if you do them*. If you don't, they don't. If you're half-assed about it, your results will be mixed. Of course, everyone is different, so some things will work for you, and some won't.

So my first request of you is to keep an open mind even if you don't think something will work for you, why not try it? As well as being a coach since 2004, I have also been coached since 2002, and I've learned to just try what my coach is asking me to do, even if I can't see how it will help (meditating to help me get through my list seemed totally counter-intuitive, and yet it works so well).

Try it. Whatever it is. Even if you're convinced that it won't work, allow yourself to experiment anyway. You never know, it might just work. And of course, feel free to make adjustments if you think a tweak will make the solution better for you. I remember hearing the advice about writing from Wayne Dyer to get up at 4am, or some other ungodly hour, and write while the world is quiet and there are no interruptions.

I am not a morning person, and I love my sleep, so this advice gets into the top 3 of advice I am least likely to follow. However, I did take on board creating a time to write and making that a time when I am least likely to be disturbed, and I tweaked the solution so that A. I'd actually do it, and B. it would work for me. And once, when I couldn't sleep, I got up at 4am and wrote…turns out Dr Dyer was right, it is a wonderful time to write. It's also a wonderful time to be asleep though, so right now it's not my usual writing time.

So if there's a suggestion in this book (or anywhere else that you are seeking answers to how to get over your obstacles) that doesn't quite fit you, adjust it. Change it so it will fit you. Change it so you will do it because it's more important that you do it than that you do it the way you were told to do it. Over a decade in business has taught me that blindly following advice without thought to your personality and your best way of working is a waste of your time and effort. You know yourself best so tailor what you see and hear to fit you.

My suggestions come from years of coaching clients to get over obstacles (and getting over obstacles myself), so I know they work, but you may need to change it up to make it work for you. Like the client who instead of meditating every day (because that's boring) instead stares out of the window and breathes deeply when her commuter train takes her through some countryside. It's the same difference, but the tweak is what makes it work for her.

Ultimately, you really want to be trusting yourself too, so if your intuition is screaming 'NO', listen to it. For the first few years of my business (when I knew nothing about running a business), I would follow advice (or try to) that made me feel sick to my stomach. I thought maybe I wasn't cut out for business. Turns out it was my intuition telling me there was a better way for me.

So trust what your gut is telling you. Just make sure it is gut instinct pulling you away, not a knee-jerk 'yeah, but' response. If you're not sure which it is, sit with it for a few minutes and notice, are your thoughts saying "yeah, but" or is your heart saying "this is not for you"?

Remember what I said about being a ninja problem solver? This will get rid of any yeah, but's because when you are determined to find a way, you do. Even if your situation is worse than someone else's, even if they don't seem to get how bad it is for you, even if a solution seems woefully inadequate for the scale of the problem you're facing.

Keep going, keep trying, keep attacking it from different angles. (And one of those angles might be to step away from it for a while and get some perspective!) Because if you don't, what's the alternative? You 'yeah, but' your way into staying stuck for the next while. Where's the fun in that? Big Dreams are calling you, and even bigger dreams will be following them, you need to find your way through the obstacle course with ease and grace and a determined grin on your face.

When you are thinking 'yeah, but' or 'my situation is different'...

- Keep an open mind and give it a try.
- Adjust the advice to fit you better.
- Trust your intuition.
- Keep trying to solve the problem.
- What else? What does your inner wisdom suggest you try?

From Start
To Finish

From Start to Finish

This first section is all about the obstacles that come up from the beginning through to the end of your Big Dream journey – from not knowing what to do to impatience; from resistance to getting stuck in an ebb. Many of these obstacles seem bigger than they really are, so once you have a strategy for navigating them, they won't be such a problem for you anymore.

Don't know what to do

This one feels like the Mount Everest of obstacles, because when you don't know, you don't know. However, it's actually one of the easiest obstacles to get over, because all you need to do is find out what to do. Simple, eh? It's not always that easy, I know that, but thanks to the internet, it's never been easier to find out anything than it is now. Auntie Google has more information about anything you could ever ask for than you could ever read. It's incredible, it's wonderful, it's magical (I grew up in the non-digital age so to me it's still amazing).

When you don't know what to do, remember that you are a creative being, you can figure this out. Everything is learnable, everything can be figured out. It's just a puzzle to be solved. It's not you being stupid, or a dipstick, or somehow defective. You don't know what you don't know. I didn't know anything about websites when I started my business but now I maintain my own site, and can build a site (thanks to WordPress, this is now very easy).

And just to reiterate that – you *are* a creative being. You are. All humans are (we come up with the most *amazingly* creative excuses for not doing stuff). You went to school and you learned stuff there (maybe you learned how to pretend to be listening to the teacher when you were actually listening to pop music on the radio, it's still useful knowledge). You've learned stuff all your life, you've figured it out. From how to drive to how to boil an egg to how to kiss. You didn't know how to do any of them until you knew.

All you need to do is put your thinking cap on and start coming up with some ideas and trying them. Many people think for about half a second, then say "I don't know". You need to give yourself a better chance than that to mull and consider and ponder. Bring your inner wisdom in – you've got access to guidance right there. Use it. Ask your heart and soul for help. If you believe, ask God, angels, Goddess, or guides for some guidance too.

Sometimes we genuinely have no clue where to go next and there are no ideas to be had. This is actually quite rare, so go back to putting on your thinking cap and let all your ideas be heard, even if they seem crazy. But if you've been mulling and pondering and considering for a while and you have no clue, find someone who's done what you want to do and ask them.

Auntie Google, a friend, someone you vaguely know that you think might be able to help. The worst they can do is say no. You'll be no worse off, but they might help you get unstuck. Like magic! Other people are brilliant, you know, and they know stuff. And most people are happy to be helpful.

Auntie Google has been my trusted business colleague for years. Whenever I get stuck on a business issue, off I go to Auntie Google where I either find a breadcrumb to help me in my search, or someone who can do it for me, or the answer I need to do it myself. It's not always "Ask the question, immediately get the right answer"; sometimes it takes a bit of breadcrumb following, some trail following, some changing the language because "that thing that helps search engines find your site" is not quite specific enough.

Most things you want to create in your life are not 100% unique – they've been done by someone, somewhere, before. If they can figure it out, so can you. Which brings me to my last point: no one is born knowing it all. We all figure it out. We all get stuck and don't know what to do. Then we find out what to do next. It really is that simple.

Always remember that you are more creative, resourceful, intuitive and intelligent than you give yourself credit for, and thanks to the internet, you have access to a whole world of information, resources and people who can guide you. So you don't know what to do? Go find out!

When you don't know what to do:

- Give yourself some time and space to think about what you need to do next. Write down any ideas that come to mind and keep mulling.

- Connect to your inner and higher guidance and ask for help.

- Ask someone for help – Auntie Google, a friend, a random acquaintance, anyone you can think of.

- Remind yourself that you are creative, intelligent, intuitive and resourceful. If you don't know what to do, you'll figure it out and have fun doing so.

- What else? What does your inner wisdom suggest you try?

Never getting started and not taking action

Aah, the joys of a dream; what fun to imagine living on that beach, writing that book, creating that business, moving to the farm in the country. Such fun to imagine what we want in life, but then when we think about turning the romantic ideal into reality, suddenly it feels like work, or we don't know what to do. Or it seems too big, or impossible. Or we don't have time or money or space or support. So many things can get in the way of the dream it's no wonder so many of us never seem to get started or take any action.

So, if you're struggling with this one, please know that you are not alone. Many people that I've coached over the years have found themselves just not getting started or not taking the action they need to. The good news is, it's a fairly easy one to fix. All you need to do is to start, and to take action. Yes, I know that sounds too simplistic, and if it was that easy you'd have done it already, but once you've taken that first step, continuing is easier.

One easy way to get started is to find the feeling behind what you want, and do what you can to feel that feeling now. So if you want the farm in the country for the freedom and connection to nature, what can you do today to feel free, how can you connect to nature today? For example: dance like no one is watching, change your routine, listen to the birds sing, watch the sun set.

We want most things because we think they will make us happy. So what can you do to make you happy today? What would be fun, what would bring you joy? Get happy. It's way easier to get started and to take action when you're feeling good, so make feeling good a high priority. Why wait until you get your dream before you start feeling happy and enjoying your life? Enjoy the journey, even if you don't feel like you're making much progress toward the destination!

Then do something, anything. Start anywhere. Take one action. It doesn't have to be a big action. In fact, it's probably easier if you make it a teeny, tiny, easy baby step. Don't get paralysed by indecision, just pick something to do and do it. Don't worry about it being a good action, a right action, a perfect action…just do something, anything. It really doesn't matter what you do, what matters is that you do something.

Often when you start moving, you'll keep moving, like a ball rolling down a hill. If you still feel like you're not getting started or taking action, or you keep stalling, explore what's behind the inaction. Not getting started or not taking action are often symptoms of a different obstacle – perhaps a fear, perhaps not wanting what you thought you wanted, perhaps an issue of time or money or not knowing what to do.

Take some time to consider what's really going on, what's getting in the way. Please don't panic about this – there could be 15 obstacles stopping you getting started or stopping you taking action, but all of them are fixable. You can get over, under, round or through them all. Also, most of the time, busting past one obstacle makes the others easier to navigate, or they might all just fall down. Imagine knocking down a wall – you don't have to hit every single brick. Just start whacking with the sledgehammer and you'll find that one brick will take several others with it.

Whatever you do, keep doing something. Find a place to begin, and after every action, ask yourself what's next, what's next, what's next? An object in motion tends to stay in motion. An object at rest tends to stay at rest. So keep moving. I'm not suggesting you run around like a headless chicken (this also is not helpful), but take inspired action. Dig deep into your inner wisdom and higher guidance, ask for inspiration as to what to do. Then go do it. Over and over again. Action is magic.

When you are not getting started or not taking action:

- Find the feeling behind what you want and do what you can to feel that feeling now.

- Get happy now – it's easier to take action when you feel good.

- Do something, anything just to get you started…then keep moving.

- Explore what's stopping you.

- What else? What does your inner wisdom suggest you try?

Problems with finishing and following through

This obstacle was my nemesis for years. I had so many great ideas: products, books, blogs, series, lots of seriously good stuff. I was a great starter. I could start a project with ease, diving into a great idea and going for it. Then I'd get stuck. I'd get bored. I'd stop for some reason and never start again. The ghosts of projects past would haunt me, draining my energy, dulling my desire to start. What's the point in yet another unfinished project?

The main thing that turned my finishing ability around from pathetic to champion was single tasking. Doing one thing at a time. Having one project on the go at a time. You may not have to do this forever, you may find you can have a couple of things going on and still finish each one. But if you have years of unfinished business littering your past, it's time to embrace the idea of doing one thing at a time and following through until it's done.

Let's separate those two things – one thing at a time first. One project at a time. One dream at a time. One major goal at a time. Hey, if you've been doing 2000 things at once for years, and you're finishing everything, following through on every idea, you can ignore this advice. Otherwise, pick one. Any one. It could be the oldest one, the newest one, the one with the most juice and excitement for you, the one that's nagging at you to be done, or the easiest one.

It doesn't matter which one. Just pick one. I call it my Major Project. I may have a minor project or three going on at the same time, but my main focus is on the Major Project. That's the one I make sure to work on every week, at least once a week. Diary allowing, I'll work on it every day, even if I only do 15 minutes on it. Before I started single tasking, I wrote 2 books and one journal in 7 years. Since, I have completed 3 books, 3 courses, and the Beach Cards in 3 years.

Twice as much in half the time. Are you convinced about single tasking yet? Once you've picked your ONE project, dream or goal, it's time for part 2: follow it through until it's done. Show up to it, day after day after day. If you want to write a book, show up, sit your ass down and write, day after day after day. I know that's boring for the starters among us, but it's how shit gets done, by showing up and working on it, day after day after day.

By all means find your best way to do that – if chipping away doesn't work well for you, clear your calendar and deep dive into it for a week at a time. Experiment with what following through looks like for you. Try different things. Find productivity tips and try them out. Ride Wild Donkeys, use the Pomodoro technique, do your most important tasks first, or just keep swimming[1]. Find a way to stick to the task at hand. A way that works for you and ideally, that you enjoy. That may mean involving someone else to do the bitty, annoying, finicky finishing bits!

There are times when a project, an idea, a dream, or a goal will need to be put on hold for a while. I am not suggesting you push through regardless of your inner wisdom telling you to pause or wait. However, if you pause, do so with full consciousness that this project or dream is being deliberately put on the back burner for now, and keep testing the water to see if it's time to pick it back up again.

When you're a starter, you'll know the joy that comes from starting something, from diving into a project, from starting the journey to a dream or goal. Ah, the bliss. It's such fun, right? Here's the interesting thing:

Finishing is WAY MORE FUN!

I love to start stuff. I am an inspiration junkie, and I love, love, love following my inspiration wherever it leads. I'm happy to have a go and try something new. Even better is completing things. Even better is looking at the products and books I've created and seeing them DONE. Even better is knowing that I did that. Even

---

[1] For more on each of these techniques, check out this blog post where I share my experience of them all: http://www.donnaonthebeach.com/blog/get-shit-done/

better is crossing the actual finishing line. Even better is knowing that many of the ideas I have now WILL be completed.

Starting gives you a high, but it's a short lived high, like a caffeine-shot of energy that disappears within hours, leaving you needing more. Finishing gives you a lasting high…like the energy you have from being healthy and active. It lasts. It's always there. Whereas the joy of starting is replaced by the drudge of following through all too soon, finished is finished forever. It's fabulous. Once you've done it, it's done. That achievement can be hung on your wall forever. You can stand tall and say 'I did that'.

Remember the lasting joys of completion next time you find yourself being distracted away from your Major Project by a new, bright, shiny object. Becoming a finisher is not always easy, but it is possible. I know, I've done it, and I've helped several clients who were constantly starting new things to learn to become finishers. It takes time, it takes practice, but it is your choice to learn to be a finisher…or not.

So make the choice to do it. Make the choice to complete something, anything. Then do it again and again and again until you find you don't have 6 million things unfinished and you are a champion finisher.

When you are not finishing and following through:

- Single task.

- Stick to the task – show up day in, day out.

- Remember the joys of completion when you're being tempted by something new.

- Become a finisher, by finishing stuff.

- What else? What does your inner wisdom suggest you try?

Impatience

Sometimes when I am talking to people about what they want for their life, they are so frustrated, and they want it NOW! I can certainly appreciate that sentiment. I am horribly impatient by nature, but what I've learned over many, many years of trial and impatient error is that trying to rush things because of impatience doesn't work well.

Impatience and frustration do not get you closer to where you want to go. In fact, they get you further away (I know this, I've experimented at some length and it definitely takes you further away from what you want). I'm a big believer in allowing yourself to feel how you feel, so I am not going to ask you to *not* feel impatient or frustrated.

That would also not work. You feel frustrated and impatient, that is just how you feel. Feel it, write it, move it, sing it, dance it, scream it. Vent it, let go of it. Clear it before you do anything else, or you'll be working from some really hinky energy. We have a tendency to jump into action or over-react when we're feeling impatient or frustrated, and our choices aren't always good when we come from impatience. Better to clear that energy first before you do anything.

Ironically, impatience doesn't get you moving forward faster. More haste, less speed right? The tension created by your impatience makes it hard to flow forwards, gives you ulcers and puts utterly unnecessary and unhelpful pressure on you. So slow down. (I know you're probably hating this advice, but trust me when I tell you slowing down will get you there faster). Breathe. Centre yourself.

Get into the state of calm and peace – this is more productive than running round like a headless chicken trying to make things happen, or worse, complaining about things taking forever without actually trying to do anything at all. Once you're calm(er), check in with your inner wisdom...what is this impatience trying to tell you? Be present with what you're feeling. It's a sign of something, figure out what. Instead of being ruled by your impatience, listen to it.

When you start to feel antsy about everything taking so damn long, do whatever your inner wisdom suggests will curb the impatience. Impatience and frustration are great signposts to show you there is something to do, to change or to prioritise. You can either just feel impatient and frustrated and angry and down on yourself and like you are not getting anywhere, OR you can USE that feeling.

Find out what it is telling you. Find out the positive intention of that feeling. Find out how it can help you and serve you and use it to get closer to your Big Dream instead of further away. I've found that when I'm feeling impatient and frustrated, it tends to point to something I am not doing or working on. Once I take some action, however small, the impatience subsides. Impatience tells me what I need to make time for or make more important.

And finally, check your self-care. I'm going to estimate that 70% of the time for my clients and I, impatience points to something we're not doing, something we want that we're not prioritising. The rest of the time, it's a sign that our self-care, self-love, energy and joy have slipped. These are incredibly important foundations for a calm, peaceful, happy, contented life, and so often we just don't take care of ourselves, our energy levels, or our joyfulness.

Instead we push ourselves, making ticking items off a list more important than our health – physically, mentally, emotionally or spiritually. Ironically when we are in crisis in any of those areas, we realise that no task, no event, no achievement is more important than our good health. So make sure you're listening to the signs from body, mind, heart and soul...and impatience or frustration can be one of those signs. When you're taking excellent care of yourself, you may find your impatience just disappears.

When you're feeling impatient:

- Vent your frustration and impatience.

- Slow down.

- Listen to your inner wisdom, and pay attention to what your impatience is telling you.

- Check your self-care, self-love, energy and joy.

- What else? What does your inner wisdom suggest you try?

Everything taking longer than you expect

This is a weird one but one that I am often tripped up by. It's not exactly an obstacle as such, it's more a weight tied to your legs that slows you down and gives other obstacles a chance to catch up with you and attack. Many of us are prone to underestimating how long everything takes, especially when it comes to creating a fabulous life.

After all, we see all these other people doing things in a snap of a finger, right? Only they don't. We just see them when they arrive on our radar as a writer, singer, businessperson, or beach bum. We don't see the years up to that point when they were quietly writing, singing, entrepreneuring and looking for their beach. We don't see how long it actually took to get to where they are.

There are times when *you* are slowing things down (often by huffing and puffing about things taking so damn long), but sometimes it is just a matter of resetting your expectations. I remember talking to a business coach about how badly my business was doing after 5 years. He laughed out loud and said to me, "Donna, your business is still a small child. Let go of the expectation that you *should* be further along and be where you are."

Excellent advice. It is advice I hand to you too. You are where you are. Things take as long as they take. When I wrote my first book in 2014, I wasted a lot of time worrying about how long it was taking me (because somehow my expectation was a time-scale of months, not years). Then I read somewhere that big publishers have time-scales for editing, formatting, marketing and releasing a book of 12-18 months minimum.

Expectation reset! There are authors (and I'm sure, publishers) who publish faster than I do, but what they do isn't really my business. If someone else started a business in 40 seconds, or wrote a book in an afternoon, or paid off their debts in a week, that means nothing – you will do it in your time. It will take as long as it takes, no matter what expectations you have.

If you are aware that you tend to underestimate the amount of time things take, either release your expectations altogether and just wait and see how long it actually takes, or quadruple the amount of time you expect it to take. I did this on a project I was working on, and it actually took even longer! My original estimate had been nearly 5 times shorter than the time the project actually needed.

Sometimes it's not about your expectations as much as your focus. If you're working on 88 things at once, it will take longer to see any progress on any of them than if you focus your attention and single task. Have a single project on the go (or one major project and one or two minor projects), work on one thing at a time, and stop having 56 windows open on your computer.

Since I've been doing this, I've got so much more finished. Previously I'd have had 12 projects on the go at once and got nowhere with any of them. I feel like I've accelerated from 2 to 100 miles an hour, just by focusing on one thing until it's complete. Single tasking is brilliant for making real progress.

Lastly, check whether you are slowing yourself down for some reason. The release of my first book took much longer than expected (by months). This was partly because I decided I was done long before I really was done, and I went and started a new project, thereby cutting the time I could spend on finishing the book in half. It was also partly because I found the finishing bit tedious so I kept putting it off. And finally, it was partly because fears and doubts were raising their heads.

The end of a project is a prime time for fear and stress to appear, because suddenly it's all becoming very real. Obstacles may appear, you may start putting obstacles in your own path, it's a perfect moment for some self-sabotage. If you find yourself getting in your own way, firstly DO NOT criticise yourself for it – it is what it is, beating yourself up won't help you fix it.

Simply notice what is going on, and why. Then change something, do something to make it easier for yourself to cross that finish line. One of my clients found she'd taken her foot off the gas at the end of her project because it was nearly done. Only there was still quite a lot to do. Once she started putting more time and effort in again, progress was quick and the project was completed. Simply find a solution to whatever problem is causing you to slow yourself down.

And if you're not slowing yourself down…just keep swimming. Things take as long as they take, so keep going. The end of a project, goal or dream can be the hardest part…when you feel so close yet so far from the top of the mountain. Nevertheless if you just keep climbing, you *will* reach the summit.

When everything is taking longer than you expect:

- Remember that things do take time, so relax and be where you are.

- Reset your expectations.

- Single task.

- Check if you have been slowing yourself down somehow, and if so, make an adjustment. If not, just keep swimming.

- What else? What does your inner wisdom suggest you try?

Haven't done it yet syndrome

I was talking to a client this week about doing something they have wanted to do for years, and haven't done anything with yet. When we started to discuss what was in the way, this lovely obstacle raised its head "I haven't done it up until now". I love this obstacle, it's just so sweet! You know: pretty, colourful, no nutritional value at all.

Seriously, there's nothing to this obstacle – it's sleight of hand, it's a mirage, it's not real. There's no substance to it whatsoever. Yesterday I hadn't driven a certain way home from Birmingham Heartlands Hospital. Today, I did. The fact that I hadn't ever done it before had zero bearing on whether I could do it today.

Just because you have never done something in the past doesn't mean you can't do it now.

I do understand this self-imposed limitation. So do elephant keepers. When elephants are babies, keepers will tie them to a stout post which they can't pull down, because they are small. When they're big, they have learned that they can't pull down the post, so they don't try. The bitter irony is of course, that a full-grown elephant can easily escape.

It's called Learned Helplessness. Animals (and we) learn that they cannot do something, or there are unpleasant and painful consequences for trying. So they don't try anymore. However it's not necessarily true that we can't do it today – we may have grown into a big elephant in the meantime.

Let the story of yesterday go – you didn't do yoga, or write, or read, or meet your friends as often as you'd like. Talking about not having done it doesn't help you get it done. Focusing on the fact you've not done it simply makes you feel bad, inadequate, and lazy. It doesn't move you forward – unless you're looking at why you haven't done it.

So check why you haven't done whatever it is. Is it because you were a small elephant who couldn't move the post? Is it because your laptop was broken and needed to be fixed first? Is it because you weren't ready yesterday? Is it because the last 6 months of yesterdays were just too busy? Is it because you forgot? Is it because you were just too tired? Is it because you didn't know where to start?

Even when you look at the why's, they are often past why's. For example, if you haven't done something because you forgot about it. All you can do in that instance is remind yourself of it, and if you're thinking of it now, you're reminded. Now crack on and <u>do</u> the thing that you've been not doing! The cure for this learned helplessness is action. So take some action! DO something.

But just before you do…check. Do you actually want to do this thing? Because sometimes the reason we didn't do something yesterday was because we didn't want to. One of my clients was told by a previous coach that she needed a book for her business, so she hired me to help her get it written. There was one minor problem: she didn't want to. Writing is not her thing. So I coached her to find a different way to showcase her work and to stop beating herself up for not doing stuff she just didn't want to do.

If you do want to do whatever you didn't do yesterday, figure out your next step and take it. If you don't know what to do, figure out what to do next, just get into some action. Then tomorrow you won't be able to say "I haven't done it yet"! Unless it genuinely is impossible (as in no one, anywhere, ever, has done that thing), take some action to make what you hadn't done yesterday something you've now done.

Before I went to Australia, I'd never been to Australia, travelled alone, backpacked, slept in a dormitory as an adult, or eaten Moroccan food. Before I started a business, I'd never started a business, created a website, written a blog or recorded a podcast. Before I wrote a book, I'd never written a book, edited a book, formatted a book, held a book I'd written in my hands, or seen my dad sell my book.

Before you've done whatever it is you want to do, you won't have done it. It means nothing that you haven't done it yet. Do it now. Take your past lack of action and learn from it, take past failures and learn how to succeed. Go and do whatever it is you want to do. Just take one teeny tiny baby step – then you'll be a step closer to it than you were yesterday. Make the decision now not to let your past inaction dictate your future.

When you're suffering from haven't done it yet syndrome:

- Forget yesterday. So you didn't do it then. So what?

- Check the why's. Why didn't you do it? Is there a reason you didn't do it? If so, learn from that, fix the problem and crack on!

- Check that you want to do the thing you haven't done. If not, go do something else. If you do...

- Take some action. Figure out what's next, figure out a baby step and do that.

- What else? What does your inner wisdom suggest you try?

Resistance

Ever feel like you're pushing a rock up a hill, through treacle, with steel boots on? Yeah, that's what resistance feels like. Even though you know you want to do something, go somewhere, make a change, there's this damn resistance stopping you. The first thing to note about resistance is that it's rarely just resistance that is the issue here. Resistance is almost always a symptom rather than the true issue. So you need to dig deeper. WHY are you resisting doing, changing, trying?

The answers may not be obvious, and you may need to give this one the gift of some time and space to think. I know you're busy and important and just need to get on with it, but taking a few minutes out to ponder the roots of your resistance will move you forwards far faster than continuing to push that rock uphill, through treacle, with steel boots on. Simply ask "why am I resisting?" and allow yourself to access the answers.

Trust yourself to know what's going on. You may want to talk it through with a trusted friend or coach, you may want to write it out. One of my clients decided to write about her resistance, because no answers were coming up (resistance was blocking them, ironically). After some time of struggling to figure out why she was resisting change in her life, she wrote "I don't understand why I'm resisting this…" and the answer came out of her pen…fear of change, pure and simple.

The answers are there, you just need to find them. While you're at it, look for the positive intention of the resistance. There is always a positive intention to the things we do even when it looks like we're getting in our own way. Often it is to keep us safe or to protect us, so find the positive intention of your resistance. Once you know what that is, you can either soothe that part of you that wants to keep you safe, or find a new way to protect yourself from failure. For example, by failing with gusto and enthusiasm.

Resistance can sometimes be a really positive reaction. For example, one of my clients was resisting expanding her business, taking on staff, renting premises. She realised that her original plan had been for the business to enable her to travel the world, and this new expansion plan - while the next sensible, logical step - would actually take her further away from what she really wanted; the freedom to travel.

So check you're not resisting because you just don't want what you are trying to do or change. We're so quick to assume there is something wrong with us, or we're self-sabotaging or some such guff. What if you trusted yourself? What if you trusted that you were doing what's right for you? Even if it looks like you are holding yourself back, what if your actions are actually wise and right?

I've often had this when I'm trying to do something a really complicated way. I'll resist and resist and resist, and then I'll realise there is a much easier way to do what I wanted to do. My resistance was actually saving me time (and in some cases, money). Trust yourself. Trust that you do the things you do for good reasons. If you knew that you were always acting in your best interests, what would this resistance be showing you?

When you're resisting:

- Find the root cause of the resistance.

- What's the positive intention of resisting?

- Check you really want what you are reaching for.

- See if there is a better way to do what you want to do.

- What else? What does your inner wisdom suggest you try?

Getting ahead of yourself

This is a really common obstacle, and most of the time people don't even realise they are actually getting in the way of doing what they want to do. They think they are planning, being smart, organising themselves to make that dream happen, but actually they are putting a huge roadblock in their own path.

Take this example from one of my clients: "I haven't started advertising my business yet because I need a website, business cards, a business plan, a business bank account, a Facebook page, a blog, a book, a twitter account, an Instagram account..." The list went on and on and on. I replied "or you could just start telling people what you're up to and get some clients? The other stuff will come...or not." (Because I know several people with successful businesses and none of that stuff!)

This client could have spent another year or three getting the so-called essentials in place when actually the only thing a business needs is a paying client. All the other stuff is optional. When you're at the start of a Big Dream like writing a book or starting a business, what you tend to see as you look at others with that dream is the end product – the published book, the established business with website and social media and snazzy cards.

But the truth is you need to start at the beginning, not the end. Simplify instead of complicating. Get on with it instead of putting it off. I get it, I've done it...that's why I'm saying DON'T DO IT! It doesn't help you at all, it delays your journey, distracts you, takes you away from the thing you really want, and in some cases puts you off altogether.

I have lost count of the number of people who've asked me about writing books, and they're worried about the formatting. Write the book first. Or they're worried about who'll publish it. Write the book while investigating publishers. Or they want to know how to get it on Amazon. Write the book first. Here's what I know: the people who wrote the book are the ones who formatted and got published and have books on Amazon. The people worrying about those things often haven't written a word.

It's so easy to get ahead of yourself, get totally overwhelmed and find that you've made zero progress on your Big Dream for years on end. So check, do you really need the business paraphernalia? Maybe if you are planning an internet business, you need a website, but to begin with perhaps you only need one page. Simplify your planning, make it easy for yourself to actually do it, and question your assumptions about what you need to do.

My client had never considered that she could just tell friends about what she was up to and start the business without so much as a hint of the bells and whistles she thought she needed. There are many experts out there who will tell you that you have to have the latest social media or technology or branding or logos to successfully do anything at all.

It ain't necessarily so.

Maybe you believe you need a publisher before you write a word. What will the publisher need from you? At least the concept, at least an outline, possibly even the first chapter and the synopsis? So crack on with writing!! If you know that a specific publisher that you really want to be signed by has a procedure to follow, there is nothing wrong with following that procedure. Just don't pause your dreams indefinitely while you're doing that.

There is a big difference between a bit of planning and getting ahead of yourself. Planning is good. Being aware of what's coming is useful. Knowing you will need an editor is good to know. Worrying about editing a book before you've written a word is a waste of your time. Learn the difference – one is more about awareness, research and possibly some preparation. The other is paralysing and actively gets in the way of what you want to do.

Personally, I'm not a huge fan of planning anymore. I did it for my business – most of the plans went sideways. I did it for my book – I was still woefully unprepared for what it entailed. (I thought a month was a reasonable amount of time to edit, format and publish my book. Publishers take 6-18 months to do the same. D'oh!) To be honest, I usually wish my planning had been better when I get to each milestone. But here's the thing I've learned...

You can figure it all out when you get there.

When you get to the point you genuinely need business cards or an editor, you'll figure it out. When you need to format your book or create a website, you'll figure it out. When you come across something you don't know how to do, you'll figure it out. When your carefully laid plans go totally awry, you'll figure out what to do now. When you come across something you hadn't considered in your plan, you'll figure it out.

When the research you did last year is now out of date, you'll figure out what is possible now. The rapid pace of technology means that if you learn something new this year, by next year it will have changed. You'll figure it out. That's what we do, us humans. We're very clever like that. Trust yourself to be smart and resourceful and creative, and to figure it out when you get there.

So you've realised you've got way ahead of yourself...what do you do now? Here's the really simple antidote: Get back into this present moment. What's next? What's the next itty bitty, teeny tiny, baby step? Go do that. Write a sentence of your book. Tell someone about your business. Do the very next thing in front of you. Simplify it as much as possible, and then keep taking the action you need to take now and let the future take care of itself.

When you're getting ahead of yourself:

- Check if you need what you think you do or if you can simplify matters.

- Learn the difference between planning and getting ahead of yourself.

- Trust yourself to figure out what you need when you need it.

- Come back to the present moment...what do you need to do next?

- What else? What does your inner wisdom suggest you try?

Biting off more than you can chew

If you're anything like me, you tend to think you can take on way more than is physically possible for any human who wants to keep her sanity. It's a new global disease – busyness is an epidemic; having it all is something we're all trying to chase. Unfortunately, having it all can mean relentless action to maintain it all.

And this can end up being completely self-defeating, because rather than admit we've bitten off more than we can chew, we just carry on, pretending to be superwoman and drowning in too damn much to do. I know, I've done it myself fairly regularly. What my comprehensive experiments in this area have taught me is that when you bite off more than you can chew, you choke.

Drowning in too much to do is no fun, and it's also tremendously inefficient. Stress and over-busyness are not the best ways to get more done. Remember the hare and the tortoise? The tortoise wins because he slowly, inexorably and calmly keeps on moving. The hare dashes about in a hundred different directions, gets all stressed out and winded and fails to reach the end.

I know it seems sexier to be the hare – to be the one who wears her stress like a badge of honour, to be the one everyone else is in awe of for having so much on your plate. Only most of the time, you are a basket-case inside. It takes a tremendous amount of energy to keep up the facade of having it all together when behind the scenes you're falling apart.

Ugh. Truly, forget about looking like you're superwoman. No one is, and it's just too much like hard work. When you've bitten off more than you can chew, admit it. You're not superhuman, you're drowning and it's time to change something. Usually when we've been trying to do more than is possible, we let our self-care slip in favour of pushing, working, doing, trying, exhausting ourselves. An interesting habit, but really a very destructive one.

So once you've admitted you've taken on too much – check up on your self-care. How cared for are you feeling right now on a scale of 1-10? If it's less than a 7 (and that's likely when you're doing too much), what can you do right now to take care of you? Bearing in mind that if you break down, there's no going to the shops and getting a new you. Take the time to give yourself what you need, and start to feel good – the better you feel, the easier life is.

Once your self-care is improving, take a deep breath and slow down. Slowing down actually helps you to speed up. When you are relaxed, working in manageable bites and at a reasonable pace, you can actually do more than when you're stressed and flying at breakneck speed. Also, when you're moving slowly enough for calm reflection, it is easier to see what tasks can wait, what is truly urgent, and what doesn't need doing at all.

One December, I had a to-do list that would have taken me 2 months to complete, and I was trying to do it all in about 16 working days. Impossible. I was so busy trying to get through the endless to-do's and panicking about how much I had to do that I couldn't see the true priorities. Once I slowed down (after a slight meltdown), I realised that 75% of the list didn't have to be done before Christmas.

So let yourself slow down and calmly decide your priorities. Once you have, start figuring out exactly what's next, rather than trying to do everything at once. By all means, note down things that will need to be done in future, but then put them out of your mind and focus only on what's next. To take this even further, break each task down into baby steps (something that can be done in 10-15 minutes).

If you get into the habit of doing this, it actually helps you to stop biting off more than you can chew because you are more level-headed and pragmatic about what can be done in the amount of time you have. It also keeps you more rooted in the present, instead of off in future stresses. You can only do one thing at a time anyway, so pick what's next, break it into easily manageable pieces, and just keep going – easily and calmly.

When you've bitten off more than you can chew:

- Admit you've bitten off more than you can chew.
- Take a look at your self-care – what can you do to feel more cared for right now?
- Slow down and take stock.
- Find the next step and break that down to a baby step. Repeat.
- What else? What does your inner wisdom suggest you try?

The contraction after the expansion

There's a phenomena that happens just after something amazing happens, or as you're expanding into a new way of being, where you contract, where lots of fear and worry and doubt and stress suddenly come up (or you just want to fall on your face with exhaustion and stay there for the foreseeable future). This is normal. It's nothing to worry about. It's like the exhale after the inhale, the ebb of a wave after it's crested, the hangover after a big night out.

It also sucks, big time.

For years I thought it was just me, that maybe I was crazy-pants or something. For years I would worry about it and stress more because this contraction was happening, thereby extending the contraction and almost cancelling out the expansion. The first time I heard someone talk about this, I nearly fell off my perch. It's a thing; it's not just me! Thank God. I'm not crazy-pants (well, not over this anyway). Other people experience it too.

It still sucks though.

But it is actually a neurological process, explained by science. The gist is this: with new thoughts and experiences, you create new neural pathways, but there comes a point where the brain freaks out and says, 'Stop! Let's go back to comfortable, well-worn pathways', and you get all the stress and exhaustion and backlash from your success.

This is actually a good thing and shows the changes you are going through. The very fact that you are getting to the edge of your comfort zone means you are changing, things are moving for you. That's fantastic! And if you can stay calm and not dive into the fear and doubt and stress and exhaustion, the contraction will pass, and you'll be able to get back to the fun stuff you were up to when it arrived.

So, when your next contraction arrives, don't panic! Remind yourself it is natural and normal – so much so that it is studied by neuro-scientists. Breathe, slow down, and take the opportunity to pause. If you're expanding, you have probably been doing things differently so take a moment to regroup, to consider how far you've come. If you're halfway up the mountain, this is the moment to stop and have your sandwiches and take in the view.

While you're pausing, check in with your body, mind, heart and soul (especially body and mind because they're often the parts of you most affected by expansion) to see how you're feeling and what you can do to feel better. If you're exhausted, rest. If you're stressed, meditate, sleep or take time off. If you're worried, distract yourself from those worries, dance them off or write them out.

If doubts are running rampant, up your self-care and self-love to counter those doubts. If fears are coming up, be gentle with yourself, up your self-care and self-love and let them pass by. Be aware of what you feel and what you need, and give yourself the care, attention and TLC you need.

Ultimately, the best way to deal with a contraction is to go have some fun and wait for it to pass. It will. And the less significance you give this pull-back, the quicker it will pass. It's so tempting to go into panic mode, to think that everything is falling apart, to decide that all the good work you've done has been for nothing and life's never going to damn well change for you. But wait! Go have some fun and wait...if this is the contraction after the expansion, it will be gone soon. If it's not, fun won't do you any harm as you're figuring out your next moves.

When you're experiencing the contraction after the expansion:

- Don't panic! It's natural and normal and explained by neuro-science, no less.

- Breathe, slow down, take this opportunity to pause.

- Listen to the messages of your body and mind – check in with what you need and give yourself that care and love.

- Go have some fun and wait for the contraction to pass.

- What else? What does your inner wisdom suggest you try?

Getting stuck in an Ebb

So, there's a natural ebb and flow to life – night and day, wax and wane, the seasons throughout the year and this reflects in our energy and life too. Sometimes we're flowing forward, easily moving, and feeling fabulous about life and our Big Dreams and goals. Sometimes we feel like we're pushing against an immovable wall, getting nowhere fast and feeling terrible about it to boot.

We're not quite in total meltdown, more in purgatory. It's not a contraction after an expansion (although the two can look similar), and you feel like you've been going backwards or going nowhere for a while. Ebbs can last for what feels like forever, like winter, and they often feel like they're lasting too damn long. (Like winter always does to me.) But they're a natural part of life, business, creativity, love, and every other journey.

With no ebb, there will be no flow. If you're like me, you will want to fight that ebb tooth and nail, but this just makes it last longer. Imagine if we tried to stop the tide from ebbing…it wouldn't work. It would be exhausting and the tide would still ebb for just as long - perhaps longer, because we delayed that ebb from starting. So think about embracing the ebb. It's going to happen anyway, so why fight it?

When I first started to do this, I realised I quite like the ebb energy – it calls for contemplation, for mulling, for taking it easy, for relaxing, for sitting back, perhaps for a little lazing and napping – all things I love. So why resist so hard? Ok, I do love the flow, the activity, the forward movement, but all of that is served by an ebb. Just as we humans are able to do more when we stop and sleep for 8 hours, our life is able to flow more when we allow the ebb to be without fighting it.

The ebb is often necessary. Most of us will push ourselves too hard and too far, ignoring the body, mind, heart and soul's many messages to stop, to rest, to pause. So when you realise you're in an ebb, take it as a reminder to up your self-care and self-love levels. Be gentle with yourself, give yourself what you need, do things that nurture and support you, do some favourite things, give yourself some serious TLC.

Sometimes this alone is enough to shift us out of ebb and into flow, but don't force it. Let it happen. Let it pass. Let it be as much as you can. It's not always easy when you're stuck in an ebb, you want to just kick yourself out of it. Try to stay with it, taking care of you, loving you, allowing yourself to mull and ponder and consider and ruminate and cogitate and moodle.

While you're doing all that, you can start to look for the wisdom in the ebb. Sometimes it's simply that you needed a break from your relentless doing for a while; sometimes it's a change of direction that's calling you; sometimes it's the necessary preparation before the next big expansion; sometimes there's an easier way to do what you've been doing; sometimes it's just time for a pause.

There's usually wisdom somewhere in that ebb, something to learn, something to experience, or something to explore. So check in with your body, mind, heart and soul – what do they need from you? What do they want to tell you? What does your higher guidance (the Divine, the Universe, the Angels) suggest about this ebb? Gently seek some answers and wisdom.

Let me repeat: gently. Don't approach it with the attitude 'What the beep is going on here, and how the beep do I make it go away?'. It's tempting, and that's often how we feel when we're stuck in an ebb, but frustration and anger are usually not that conducive to finding answers. If you journal, write about it. Talk it through with a trusted friend. Meditate. Pull oracle cards. Do whatever you do to find your answers in life (or take this opportunity to try some new tools for your answer-seeking toolkit).

As much as you can, be patient. I know that's hard when you're in an ebb. I almost always struggle with ebbs, more so the longer they last and they can last for months. Yet they do pass, flow will return, the sun will come out again, and you will feel better and more energised and inspired again. In the meantime, use the opportunity to work on your self-care, self-love and connection to inner and higher wisdom.

When you're stuck in an ebb:

- Embrace the ebb.
- Up your self-love and self-care.
- Gently look for the wisdom in the ebb.
- Be patient…flow will return.
- What else? What does your inner wisdom suggest you try?

Mistaking a pause sign for a stop sign

Sometimes you need a rest from your vision, you need to step back and get perspective. This doesn't mean you abandon your vision. It means you take a break *and come back*. Sometimes we forget that last bit, and we don't come back to our Vision and keep going. Discouragement, other obstacles, life getting in the way, lack of self-care can all contribute to this obstacle, but this is one of those obstacles that is really easy to overcome.

It's simply about having awareness of what's going on, and being open to allowing yourself to take a break for a while. I've come across this most often when someone has failed, and they take that failure as a sign to stop altogether. It's not. As Peter Jones of Dragon's Den says "Failure is just feedback". Most of us fail, many of us stop (pause) at some point but then we get back on the horse.

We learn from the failure and we try again with more wisdom, more information and more experience. By all means when you fail or fall, have a break. When your heart is broken, you need time to heal. But please don't mistake a pause, a chance to heal, for a big red STOP FOREVER sign. It isn't. So you need to come back to whatever it is that you paused on. No criticism, no blame, no judgement. It's not necessary to beat yourself up for having paused.

Even if that pause is a ten year long pause. One of my clients had put his book on hold a decade ago. He had many reasons at the time to pause and he had never gone back to his book. After checking if he wanted to go back to it, he picked up where he left off. He was tempted to write it off as a regret, but he's glad he gave it (and himself) another chance.

I don't see the point in regret. We do the best we can with the circumstances we're in. Always. We make the best decisions we can. Sometimes those decisions suck, but given the same circumstances we'd probably make the same choices, so why regret it?

Having said that, if you get the chance to go back to something you paused for a few weeks, months, even years, if you're not done with it, do go back to it. You'll feel better that you saw it through – and that's way better than feeling that you left something unfinished. If you feel you should have done it, do it now or recognise that you don't want to. That's a valid choice too.

But if you let go of something altogether, do it from a place of knowing that's what's right, not from a place of having paused and never returned to finish. So when a project, a dream or a goal gets put on hold, ask why. Do you need a break? Have you hit a wall? Is there an obstacle to be dealt with? Whatever the reason, make the decision to come back and look at it again soon. (If you're forgetful like me, you can diarise it.)

I have a list of projects in a Trello board and some have been on hold for a while. When the time is right, I'll come back to them. I know why each one is paused for now: the energy isn't there, the project needs more time than I have available right now, I need more information to take the next step, I'm not ready, or something else is calling to be done first. Because I have that list of projects, I can check on it now and again and just test…is the energy returning? Am I ready now?

Because when your project, goal or dream needs a pause for some reason, there will come a time when it is ready to go again – when you're rested, or you have more time, or your confidence is higher, or you've learned a key skill you need, or you've found a mentor. So, if you have things sitting on the back burner, check them now and again to see if they're ready to be brought back to the forefront.

If you're paying attention, you'll know, because you'll be thinking about the project more, it'll be nagging at you, always at the back of your mind, calling you back to it. The next book I will be writing (after this one is released) is an idea I first had 10 years ago. This year it started constantly bothering me, nagging at me, telling me the time has finally come to write the book. So I am.

The most important thing when you have mistaken a pause for a stop sign is to be gentle with you. We often have good reasons for pausing on our projects, dreams and goals, so beating yourself up is unfair. Not to mention utterly unhelpful. It happens. It happens to us all, so when it happens to you, simply check if you're ready to pick it back up, and either leave it happily on the back burner, decide you're not going to do it at all or get on with it now.

When you are (or have) mistaken a pause sign for a stop sign:

- If you realise you've done this – no criticism, no blame, no judgement. Just git back on that hoss.

- Whenever you stop, notice why.

- Be aware of the energy flowing back into the project or dream.

- Be gentle with you, these things happen to us all. Never beat yourself up for being human. Just get going again.

- What else? What does your inner wisdom suggest you try?

Flitting from one idea to another

One of my friends has always had a hard time with me being such a flake – every time we spoke I had a new hare-brained idea, a new passion, a new obsession. I moved from accountancy to IT, I ran off to Australia for a year, I started a journalism course (I sucked), I decided to study massage therapy, I was enthused by coaching…there was always some new thing that caught my butterfly-like attention.

And he felt this was a bad thing. That I should pick something and stick to it. Uh-huh. That was never going to happen. So instead we kept having conversations where he would say "so, how's x going?" and I'd be like "oh my god, that's so last week dahling!" And his eye would start to twitch and I'd get a lecture about sticking to something.

Actually, I wasn't quite that flaky and I'd only say "that's so last week" if I was being sarcastic. Still, this is a fair distillation of 30 conversations over 4 years or so. I wasn't deliberately trying to be flaky though. I was trying to find my place in the world, and I made some mistakes. The accountancy course? Can still render me comatose with boredom just thinking about the "management information module". SNORE.

You are allowed to change your mind. Even if it means dealing with the consequences of dropping out, leaving a relationship or changing careers. Trust yourself to know the difference between being flaky and deciding something isn't for you. Other people might not get it, but they don't have to, it's not their life, it's yours. The only voice of authority in your life is your own inner wisdom.

This is about the deep knowing in your heart that this is the right thing for you. It might look like impulsive and irrational behaviour to other people, but as long as you have the courage of your convictions, their opinions are irrelevant. I do not regret stopping the accountancy course, no matter how good a job it would have led to, no matter how exasperated my colleagues and certain friends were with me, because I knew it was right for me.

You need to be able to change your mind. I don't dispute that it is good to keep your word or to follow something through, but when you are just keeping to a plan you made when you didn't know any better, that's crazy. Of course, changing your mind is always going to look like flakiness. At the time, when I was seeking my purpose and place in the world, I was also concerned that I was being flaky, but at the same time, I knew it was the right thing to do.

It was only years later, in hindsight, with the benefit of knowing my inner yes well, that I realised I wasn't being flaky at all. I was experimenting, trying new things, discarding the ones that didn't fit. How can you know what to choose without sampling some options? So one of the best things you can do is learn to hear and follow your inner yes. That inner voice that tells you what's right for you. Here's a big tip: it's not in your head.

Many of us make decisions based on thoughts – the pros and cons, the reasons, the justifications for any decision. These are distractions, often taking us away from what we know in our heart and soul. One super quick way to get in touch with your inner yes is to toss a coin…not to blindly follow the coin (unless you're not bothered either way) but to find what you truly want.

In 1999 I was trying to decide whether to go to Australia travelling or buy a house. I had lists of pros and cons, I'd asked everyone I knew for advice and I just couldn't decide. So I tossed a coin. It came up heads – buy a house (the sensible choice). I thought "best of 3…best of 5…best of 71". At some point I realised I *wanted* to go to Australia. So I did.

My inner wisdom knew all along that this was the right thing for me, but thinking about it was getting in the way. So, find ways to connect with your inner yes: listen to your body, does it tense up or relax at the thought of what you want to do; listen to your heart, does it leap or sink when you think about what you want to do; listen to your soul, does it fly or snore when you think about what you want to do?

Use guidance cards, meditate, ask for signs, visualise, journal, pray, get out in nature, connect with your higher self, connect with your angels and guides, do whatever appeals to you to find your inner voice and learn to trust it fully.

Of course, sometimes flitting is an avoidance tactic – sometimes an obstacle gets in the way and we run away from one scary thing to a new bright and shiny idea. If that's the case, you need to know that's what you're doing and fix it, but from a place of "I'm allowed to change my mind" not from a place of "I have to do this, I said I would when I was 8 years old".

Looking back at my past flitting and flaky behaviour, I can see that sometimes it was a result of obstacles: mistaking a pause sign for a stop sign; an inability to finish; fear; resistance. In fact, I could probably list about half the obstacles in this book as reasons for some flittiness, especially when it came to creative projects. So check…what's behind the flakiness? Is it inner yeses and no's, or is it something else getting in the way?

I'm less flaky than I've ever been before because I've learned to stick with things, to face obstacles head on, to come back to an idea once I've had a break from it, to finish, to face my fears and find the reasons for resistance. I love sticking with a project to completion, staying with a life choice.

I also still change my mind a lot.

When you're flitting from one idea to another:

- Relax. You're allowed to be multi-passionate, to flit and to dip your toe in many ideas before you choose what's right for you.

- Trust yourself.

- Learn to hear and trust your inner yes (and no).

- Check the flakiness isn't the result of an obstacle.

- What else? What does your inner wisdom suggest you try?

Confidence and Trust

Confidence and Trust

By far the biggest set of obstacles you will ever come across are to do with your confidence and trust in yourself. When you are confident and you trust yourself, many of the other obstacles will either be easy to navigate, or they will disappear altogether. This section covers unhelpful beliefs, common fears as well as low confidence and low self-esteem. When you truly believe in yourself and your dreams, life will be so much easier.

Beliefs that undermine you

Everyone has some of these – beliefs that undermine what you want to do and cause you to hesitate, stop and turn back when you want to move forward. You need to excavate and mine for yours and get rid of them. For example "people like me don't get to have or do X". I guarantee there is someone just like you who has had or done X, but if you have this belief you will stop yourself, you will hold back from giving it your best shot because of a belief. Not a truth, not a fact, just a belief that isn't true.

"Whether you think you can, or you think you can't - you're right." — Henry Ford

For years, people believed the world was flat. It's not. They just didn't know any better. For years, I believed that Duran Duran were the best band in the world. Then I changed my mind. Beliefs change all the time – some change with time and age, some change in an instant. Like when you meet someone who wrote a book and you realise that people who write books aren't magical and sparkly, they're just normal people who happened to write a book.

Beliefs can be insidious little buggers who hide behind one another – they're like weeds – you pull up one, thinking that's it, but if you haven't pulled up the root, it'll be back, perhaps with a different face on. They can be a blasted nuisance. Nevertheless, just as you can make your life better by eliminating obstacles, getting rid of unhelpful beliefs will also improve your lot.

If you believe you can't write a book or start a business or run a marathon or travel the world, you will either find it harder to do it or you won't try at all. So you need to find the beliefs that don't support your dreams and zap 'em, so you can move forward with confidence.

Often a belief will be formed based on experience, but just because your business failed or your book flopped or someone didn't appreciate you yesterday, that does not mean you cannot succeed in every way today. Beliefs form from all directions – society, friends, family, our own lives, and we cannot stop these weeds from ever growing. Like every vigilant gardener knows, you have to keep an eye out for weeds or they will take over and kill the healthy plants.

In this case, the healthy plants are the beliefs that do support your vision – don't let the ivy of unhelpful beliefs take hold and kill the mighty oak. Get your axe out and chop the ivy off the tree. I could write a whole book on the subject of limiting beliefs alone, there's so much to be said about it. Happily, Auntie Google has a wealth of information on the subject. So if you want to do some work on your limiting beliefs, google "limiting beliefs" and check out some of the excellent articles and resources on the subject.

Go on a journey of exploration to find your limiting beliefs. What do you believe about yourself, the way life is, or about having what you want? Find the beliefs that might get in your way. E.g. I am not good enough, people from my background don't X, having a great life is a nice dream, but it's not real. One way to find these beliefs is to write about how you feel about having dreams come true, living a happy life, success, money, etc. and pick out anything that isn't positive and empowering.

Another good way to uncover limiting beliefs is to ask yourself why you can't do something – why you can't travel the world, start a business, write a book, and check if those *reasons* are true, or if they are limiting beliefs (they might feel true…that doesn't make them fact). Sometimes we're not the best people to spot our limiting beliefs, because we believe them! So you may want to involve friends or a coach to help you find beliefs that aren't supporting you and your dreams.

Once you've found a few thoughts, start questioning them – where did they come from? Have you heard, seen or experienced this? Have you picked it up from someone you know? Is it what society believes? Did it come from your childhood? Have you made it up to protect yourself? Get to the roots of the beliefs. This can be a really eye-opening process, and send a pile of limiting beliefs tumbling to the floor at once when you realise they're just not yours.

Do whatever you can to get rid of those beliefs that are holding you back from living the life you want to live. There are so many great ways to do that, and Auntie Google will help you with that search, but my favourites are: The Work by Byron Katie and a process of reaching for a better belief.

To give you an example of this: If I believe that I can't do something, a better belief might be "maybe I can". Even better might be "I could try". Better still might be "X has done it…so if they can, I can". Take your limiting belief and think of something a bit better, and a bit better, and a bit better. It takes just a few minutes, and if you keep doing it regularly, you will find your disempowering beliefs start to change over time. The process is explained in depth with lots of examples in "The Astonishing Power of Emotion" by Abraham Hicks.

Now, while I do believe that finding, questioning and uprooting your limiting beliefs is useful and sometimes necessary, it's not the only way to go about it. You can also choose to believe something different. Pick something you'd like to believe – like writing is easy, people like me can make their dreams come true, getting fit is fun, lovely potential partners are everywhere – and practice that belief.

Abraham-Hicks said "a belief is merely a thought you keep thinking". If you think a thought for long enough, it will become a belief that will look like a fact to you. It's not, it's just a thought you've been thinking for a long time. So think some new thoughts. Think the thoughts you want to think, think them over and over, contemplate what you might do differently if they were true. And start to replace those pesky weeds with beautiful flowers.

When you have beliefs that don't support your success:

- Find your limiting beliefs.

- Find the root. Where did this belief come from? Society? Your childhood? Your friends? Is it yours or someone else's?

- Do some weed-killing – find ways that work for you to change your beliefs.

- Plant some flowers. What would be a good alternative belief? Try that on for size.

- What else? What does your inner wisdom suggest you try?

Fear

Aaah, fear. Fear is a fabulous one. It's so big and scary and loud and really common too, like so many obstacles. Everyone has fears. I tell my clients to imagine their fears as a sleeping lion. You know that if you wake a sleeping lion, you're likely to get your head bitten off. If you wake the lion, he will roar. That's not a good thing. Your fears sleep. They are quiet and peaceful as long as you stay in your comfort zone. But get out of that comfort zone, and your fears wake up and they roar, and they bite, and they're scary. Can you see how that might stop you from going for what you want?

Let's say you want to write a book, but just the thought of sending a manuscript to a publisher terrifies you, and wakes the sleeping lion of your fears. The lion roars and bites and frightens you back into your comfort zone, and away from your dream of being a published author. The mere thought of something that far out of your comfort zone can wake the sleeping lion.

So this means many of us don't try, we don't take any action, because we don't want to get our heads bitten off. We don't want to wake that sleeping lion. We don't want to wake the fear, so we stay comfortable. Or sometimes we try to take huge leaps into the future of our dreams, but if that huge leap falls just a little short, we end up scaring ourselves back into the centre of our comfort zone. Sometimes the roaring lion scares us so much that we never want to come out of the comfort zone again. It's totally understandable, right?

But that means our dreams stay as dreams, they can never become reality because we cannot take the scary action that would wake the sleeping lion, right?

Wrong.

There is another way.

Baby step and tiptoe past that sleeping lion.

You don't have to take the big leap. You don't have to make the grand gesture. In fact, when you break it down, the thought of sending the book to the publisher is really premature. Even if your manuscript is written, it's premature. Many times the manuscript isn't even written yet, so it's laughably early to start getting scared by the roar of the lion.

If you find yourself getting stuck at making your Big Dream come true because of fear, try this: baby step. A baby step is something that can be done in just a few minutes. It's research which publishers I might contact, it's write a draft of my cover letter, it's buy some envelopes, it's write the address on the envelope, it's buy a stamp, and it's give it to a friend to put in the mail.

A baby step isn't scary in and of itself. You're just researching, or buying an envelope, or writing a draft. That's not as scary as *send my beloved book to a terrifying publisher*. It won't make the lion roar. He may open one eye and glare at you, but if you whistle and look nonchalant, he won't realise what you're up to until the latter steps. By which time you've already done the hard work, and the roaring is less effective.

When your momentum has carried you 95% of the way, the last and scariest steps lose some of their potential to frighten you. (And that last, very scary step can be delegated to a friend who has no problem putting an envelope in the post!)

Sometimes it can be very effective to dive into your fears – to let them speak to you, let them explain what it is they fear. This way you can see what exactly it is you're scared of. If baby-stepping isn't working very well, try exploring what your fears are exactly. Unexpressed fear can act as an excellent brake to stop you moving forward. Write them out or talk them out. Find out exactly what you're fearing.

Sometimes you'll find that the fear is ridiculous, or hugely unlikely, or a monster under the bed that turns out to be a sock when you switch on the light and take a look. Sometimes it'll be one of those *what if it all goes wrong* type fears. For which my favourite response is to say "what if it all goes right" and carry on regardless because we can't predict the future. Who knows what will happen? Try it and see. It might just work out to perfection. It might go horribly wrong…but if it does, you'll have learned something and you'll have tried. It's all good.

Occasionally you'll find your fear is raising a good point and you can do some contingency planning to ensure that the effects aren't as bad as you fear. Like making sure your bills are paid for 6 months or more before you jump into a new business venture, or taking on a side job to pay the bills so you can do the thing that's calling your heart and soul. Sometimes, even just knowing that if things don't work out you'll crash on a friend's couch, will ease the fear enough that you can just get on and do what you want to do with your life.

Whatever you do, don't let fear freeze you in place. It can, and it often does, but fear of something that might happen is usually scarier than the reality. Whatever fears you have, you'll deal with them *if* they happen. A lot of the time we're just borrowing trouble from tomorrow and fearing things that will never come to pass, but if they do, you'll figure out how to sort it out.

It's what you do. Life happens and you figure out how to deal with whatever comes up. So keep taking action despite any fears you might have and trust yourself to manage whatever consequences occur. You'll probably find that 90% of your fear is totally unfounded. Isn't that what you've found up until now? Most of the things you fear never come to pass?

So don't give those fears so much weight and significance. Don't give them so much houseroom. Fears are usually imagined worst-care scenarios, and we have such wonderful imaginations for our fears. So if that's you, why not use your imagination differently? Use your imagination to create best-case scenarios and what if this worked out scenarios instead of the ones that leave you humiliated and living under a bridge.

I know negativity is seen as more *realistic* (see the negativity chapter for my thoughts on that idea) but the truth is that if you're imagining what might happen in the future, you're making it up. Usually making it up and then intensifying the awfulness of it. Reality is often kinder than our fears. When I wrote my very first book in 2008, I had the fear that not many people would read it. That fear came to pass, but the fear of few sales was far worse than the reality – in reality I'd still written a book – woohoo!

Visualisation (imagining a positive outcome) is used by many successful athletes to help them succeed. So tune into that mental success strategy and let that wonderful imagination of yours (that's been having a field day with your fears) loose on your hopes and dreams. Just for fun. Turn the fear around, bamboozle it with potential good outcomes.

Fears are natural and normal – they come from the part of our brains tuned into the dangers of lions and tigers and bears, but you don't need to believe them or give them any importance at all. Baby step round them, process them if necessary, but mostly, treat them as the illusions they are and keep moving towards the life you want, despite your fears.

When you're fearful:

- Take baby steps – don't wake the sleeping lion, just keep tiptoeing past your fear.

- Let the fear speak, and do something to assuage your fear if necessary.

- Keep moving. Fear can paralyse you. Don't let it, just keep moving anyway, even though you're scared.

- Use your imagination for magical scenarios instead of fearful ones.

- What else? What does your inner wisdom suggest you try?

Discouragement and disappointment

Ugh. Discouragement. Awful. Disappointment. Horrible. Yep, I know you've been there. Me too. Plus every one of my friends, clients, and random Facebook acquaintances. So either my network is exceptionally unlucky, or this, like so many of the other obstacles, is normal, commonplace and not that big a deal. I don't mean to diminish your experience – discouragement and disappointment do utterly suck, but everyone experiences them at some stage.

It's not you being defective, deficient or lacking in any way. It's just an unfortunate part of the journey. Well, I say unfortunate. It's just part of the journey, and until we learn to deal with it with grace, humour, ease and lightness, it's unfortunate. Once you've been through the pattern a few times, and learned what helps, it does get easier, but it can still suck. That's ok, it means you're invested, you're committed, it means something to you.

But when you hit discouragement and disappointment, you need to stop being invested and committed for a little while – not for long, just until you get your mojo back. You need to give yourself a break and give yourself what you need: excellent self-care, gentle self-love, refuelling the energy tank and some fun and joyfulness. If you don't do that, you will continue to deplete yourself and you'll be running on zero energy and you'll be doing your work, your life and yourself a disservice.

I had a client who came to me 6 months after a big disappointment. She felt she'd failed (she hadn't, she'd just not

69

quite got the outcome she wanted) and she was totally discouraged. From that low energy, she'd kept going and trying to make things happen but it wasn't working. No big surprise, as she'd never given herself any time to get over the original disappointment. Once she took some time out and gave herself what she needed, her energy rose and she was able to see exactly where she'd gone wrong before, change it, and this time get a very different outcome.

It seems magical, but it isn't rocket science really. If you try to make things happen from a low energy, bad-feeling place, it's like walking uphill through treacle with steel boots on. If you take a break and get your self-care, energy and joy levels taken care of – alakazam! Good things can start to happen.

Energy, ideas, enthusiasm and feeling good all fuel taking great action and making things happen. Plus, when you're feeling good, it's easier to access inner wisdom, divine guidance and AHA's. AHA's don't tend to arrive when you sit with your chin in your hand moping. Or at least they don't to me. (Except maybe the AHA that I need time off to recharge.)

You may also need to get your Dream Team on the case. Your Dream Team are the people who support and encourage and love and empower you. You don't let just anyone on your Dream Team; you want cheerleaders, not pity party pals or gloomy gutsies. You want people who believe in you more than you do. You want people who are positive, optimistic and intuitive so they can help you get back in touch with your inspiration.

And once you're feeling better, all you need to do is keep going. Sometimes that feels difficult after a big disappointment, but you don't want to let something as insignificant as a huge, soul-crushing disappointment get in your way. Pick yourself up, dust yourself off and keep going for what you want. You may need to course correct, you may want to re-evaluate what you're going for, or you may want to use your discouragement and disappointment to fuel your determination and drive.

I've had my own business since 2004. I've met many a disappointment. I've got hugely discouraged an average of 3 times a year over that time, but once I take care of myself, get some cheerleading and get back on with it, hope returns, enthusiasm reappears and inspiration strikes. Always.

When you're discouraged or disappointed:

- Don't worry about it. Everyone experiences these things, it's not just you.

- Take a (short) break to have some fun, recharge your energy and take care of you. Give yourself whatever love and care you need.

- Get your Dream Team involved to inspire, encourage, love, hug, support and energise you.

- Keep going.

- What else? What does your inner wisdom suggest you try?

Failure

This leads on from the previous chapter about disappointment and discouragement, so if you haven't already, do read that one too. I wanted to give failure its own chapter because people think it's such a big, scary, horrible monster. It isn't. It's just a consequence of trying. We're all going to fail at some point, if we haven't already. So we might as well get comfortable with it.

"I never lose. Either I win or I learn." – Nelson Mandela

Going after success means risking failure. C'est la vie. It's no big deal to fail; it means you tried, you learned something new and you're closer to success. Failure is going to happen, it's going to hurt, but it's not that bad. After a few failures, you start to become more resilient to it, you get more comfortable with it, and it starts to hurt less. It can even become fuel for determination to succeed.

Most people who have achieved something have failed somewhere along the way. Winning sports people who've lost in the past; best-selling authors who've been rejected 100 times; musicians who've been dropped from contracts and gone on to do great things; business people who have failed businesses in their past (it's quite surprising how many successful business people have been through bankruptcy).

Failure for most people doesn't get played out in the public eye, you don't tend to go on to social media and share with the whole world that you suck. Whereas, when you succeed, you shout it from the rooftops. This means we get a skewed idea of failure and success. We think that life is like the X Factor and world ranging success comes in a couple of months, and we think everyone else is succeeding.

Not so. Everyone experiences failure. They just tend to lick those wounds in private. No one wants to say "hi world, I'm a failure". But failure is merely a consequence. Failure doesn't mean you've failed; the end. It just means you tried something and didn't get the outcome you wanted. Failure isn't a reflection of how great you are or on who you are as a person.

Failure isn't a reflection of your value. It doesn't mean that you suck. It doesn't mean you should forget what you're trying to do. It doesn't mean you will never succeed.

"Failure is simply the opportunity to begin again, this time more intelligently." – Henry Ford

Every time you fail you learn something new. You see how what you've done can be done better. Every business failure I've had has taught me something useful that has enabled future successes.

If you see what you're doing as an experiment, it helps make failing easier because you get to evaluate the experiment and see what worked and what needs tweaking. Experimentation is what we do as humans and it's how every great invention, and most great achievements, are created. We try, we experiment, we evaluate, we tweak, we try again and each time we get closer to success.

Seeing life as a great experiment, where you get to change the parameters and try different ways to succeed is a better way to see it than thinking the guillotine will fall if you make the slightest mistake. I had a client who had failed once and given up on her dream. I encouraged her to try again, having learned from that first experiment and next time, things worked out much better for her. She also learned that failure doesn't mean it's the end of your dreams, a valuable lesson for anyone to learn.

Although ultimately you want to get as comfortable as you can with failure, it does hurt, it does sting, and it does make you feel bad. Don't deny how you feel. You're allowed to be blue. Work on your self-care, go have some fun, mope a bit if that's what you need to do, express your disappointment and hurt – write it out, dance it off, talk about it with friends. (Make sure it's optimistic, empathetic friends you share with. You want them to understand, but not to agree with your failure-coloured glasses assessment that it's all shit.)

Failure is a sign you had a go. When you're ready, have another go, or try something else, armed with your new knowledge and wisdom. Get back on with your journey, failing again with style, grace, lightness and ease until you find the way to succeed all the time (um, I'm kidding, that's impossible!).

As one of my favourite quotes, attributed to Winston Churchill, says:

"Success is going from failure to failure with no loss of enthusiasm."

When you're failing:

- Remember that failure is simply a consequence of trying, it's not a reflection of your ability or value.

- Treat life like an experiment and learn from what didn't work.

- Let yourself recover from the disappointment of failure – take great care of yourself, be gentle with you, give yourself some tlc.

- Keep going.

- What else? What does your inner wisdom suggest you try?

When your dreams crash to the ground

Sometimes something happens that seems to take the legs from under you, sends a hurricane through the beautiful dream castle in the air that you're building and leaves it in ruins on the ground. It may be a failure, a disappointment, or even just the memory of something that didn't work out as you wanted it to. It happened to me just as I was working on this book – something reminded me of a disappointment from a year ago, and CRASH!

Suddenly all hope perished, all faith disappeared, my beautiful castle in the air was a ruin and all I wanted to do was sit and stare at the wall, or sleep to escape the hurt and pain. As tempting as it is to run from this, to avoid it, to stick a happy face sticker on and keep on trucking, it usually doesn't work. I tried a couple of things from my toolkit to cheer myself up and it wasn't happening, so I surrendered to the feelings.

I lay down and I cried, I stared at the wall, I fell asleep. I couldn't do this the whole time I felt this way because I had clients and things to do and places to be. So I did the best I could with the things I needed to do, and the rest of the time I surrendered to feeling hopeless and as if my dreams had broken. Surrendering to those feelings is usually the best way through them. They pass, it's often our resistance to them that makes them stick around for ages.

*Of course, I am not talking about deep depression or surrendering to harming yourself. * If you feel like that, please get professional help.*

While you're surrendering to how you feel, love yourself deeply. Be gentle with you, kind to you, loving to you. Give yourself what you need – flowers, a bath, a nap, time to heal. Don't isolate yourself from others unless you know that what you need most is to be alone. You may need to retreat to your cave and lick your wounds, or you may need your loved ones to tell you that you're fabulous, give you a hug and make you laugh.

Self-love is the most important and impactful thing you can do anytime you're feeling low, and especially when you are having a total meltdown and your dreams have crashed to the ground. So love yourself deeply. Do loving things for yourself. Surround yourself with things and people you love. Do things you love to do. Be wonderful to yourself.

When you're feeling like the bottom's fallen out of your world, it can be hard to encourage yourself, but if you can, do. If you can't, maybe write yourself a letter when you feel better, ready for the next meltdown. Because if you're a dreamer, more will come. Big Dreams require big faith and big belief in yourself and your dream. By their nature dreams ask us to build castles in the air so it's almost inevitable that a few crashes to earth will come with that.

I have bookmarked a little pep-talk from Jared Leto of Thirty Seconds to Mars[2]. He says a breakdown often precedes a breakthrough, and for me, this time, there was definitely wonderful insight that will help me to rebuild my castle in the air more substantially than ever.

---

[2] To find this pep-talk video, go to www.donnaonthebeach.com and search for 'Jared Leto' – you'll find the video link in any of those articles.

One thing to ensure you DO NOT do when your dreams have crashed to the ground is to make any rash decisions. Mid-meltdown it seems like a good idea to run away, to forget your dreams, to go live as a Vietnamese fisherman or an equally grand gesture. Don't do it. It's not a good time to make life-changing decisions. When you're so low that fish at the bottom of the sea would have a hard time finding you, it is not the time to make choices about your life.

Sometimes meltdowns and crashed dreams will expose something you do need to take care of, but let that decision come when you feel a little better. You will. This latest meltdown of mine lasted 36 hours. Then I started to feel better. It was a fairly short meltdown. The last big meltdown that I remember was a few years ago and it took me over a week to start feeling better.

Meltdowns do pass. The feeling that the world is coming to an end passes. Our castles in the air get rebuilt, we are the dreamers of the dreams. If you find that your meltdown is lingering, get some help, support and cheerleading. Check your toolkit for the things you do that make you feel better – music, books, nature, dancing, yoga, running, friends, family, and do the things that make you feel a little better. All you need to defeat darkness is a little light.

You don't have to come back to your dreams until you feel better. At that point, be gentle with yourself and your dreams – they may feel a bit wobbly for a little while. That's ok, it can take time for the effects of the meltdown to disappear. It's normal to experience a few aftershocks, and you may need time to rebuild your faith in what you're creating.

As you're rebuilding your castle in the air, notice what the meltdown has taught you. You may have learned something that will help you make your dreams come to pass, you may have found you need to take better care of yourself so you have the strength and energy for your dreams, or you may have discovered some support you need.

Whatever the meltdown brings you, even if that appears to be nothing but a tear trail and a few very bad days, it's not the end for your dreams. My castles in the air have crashed to the ground at least a dozen times and it's never yet been the end for my dreams. I simply rebuild the castles in the air from the ruins; often bigger and better and more robust than they were before.

When your dreams crash to the ground:

- Surrender to the bad feelings…cry, stare at the wall, have a nap, feel your hurt and anger.

- Love yourself deeply.

- DO NOT make any rash decisions at this moment…it's not the time.

- Wait for it to pass, if it doesn't in a few days, get some help, get your toolkit out and find ways to make yourself feel better.

- What else? What does your inner wisdom suggest you try?

Self-sabotage

I should start by saying that I don't like the term "self-sabotage". I know we do it, I know it exists but the term irritates me. It apportions blame, makes us victims of ourselves and doesn't help us stop it. It's not that you've turned into some kind of pushme-pullyou getting in your own way and pulling yourself apart, the sabotaging behaviour is simply pointing towards a puzzle that needs to be solved.

That said, we do self-sabotage. Sort of. The thing is, every part of every body has a positive intention. The part of us that is self-sabotaging usually has a positive intention – sometimes to keep us safe and protect us somehow, like an over-protective father who'd rather lock his daughter in a cupboard than let her go out with a boy. Or it can be that there's a better way to do things, or we're trying to do something we don't really want to do.

I know I self-sabotaged a lot in the past when I was trying to do something I didn't want to. I don't see that as sabotage. It's more self-saving - saving yourself from something you didn't want to do. Just knowing that you self-sabotage isn't enough – you need to find out why you're doing that. There's usually a good reason. That reason might not stand up to scrutiny, but it makes sense to a part of you.

Trust in yourself – you're always trying to do the best for yourself and your life, even if the consequences of that are to sabotage something you're trying to do. So explore what's behind the sabotage. Are you trying to do something you've told yourself is a good idea but that you don't really want to do? If that's the case, it's great that you self-sabotaged, you can stop and change course and do what you really want to do.

Are you trying to protect yourself? If so, you may need to remind that *inner dad of teenage daughter* that he needs to trust you to live your life, and being locked in a cupboard is far more damaging than fully living your life could ever be. What is your self-sabotage pointing to? See your self-sabotage as a sign post, not a character defect.

Also, things get labelled as self-sabotage that are not. (Another reason the term irritates me.) Any of the obstacles in this book can be mis-labelled as self-sabotage, but we're not necessarily self-sabotaging. We're just believing an unhelpful belief, or we're discouraged, or we're not trusting ourselves, or we've bitten off more than we can chew.

So it might not be a question of what's behind the self-sabotage, but a question of what obstacle is in our way that we've assumed is self-sabotage. We often jump to the conclusion that we are the problem or we are in the wrong. But often, it's not that we are at fault or defective – there's a reason we do what we do.

If you're not sure what's behind your self-sabotaging behaviour, you can often find the problem by taking some baby steps. If you find yourself sabotaging a baby step, you can more easily pin down the exact issue. If you've been sabotaging your plan for world domination, it's hard to narrow down exactly what the problem is! It could be a fear of success, a fear of failure, not really wanting the world to genuflect to you, not wanting the stress or hard work of it, all sorts of things could be obstacles to world domination.

If you just baby step, it's easier to identify the core problem(s). Also, you may find that as you take baby steps, the self-sabotaging behaviour stops. Action can be magical, after all. One of my clients came to me saying she always self-sabotaged what she was trying to achieve. She picked one goal to work on, took baby steps, and discovered fears of success, fears of being a tall poppy, discouragement, imposter syndrome…and more.

They were all hiding under the label of self-sabotage. As she took the baby steps, she noticed the obstacles coming up, but just kept going, and self-sabotage became self-awareness. It no longer stopped her from doing what she wanted; it showed her when there was something to see, something to clear, a different path to travel, or a time to get support.

Self-sabotage is a symptom. It isn't the cause of the problem – it's rare that we're just getting in our own way from malice and spite. It's not that you're naughty or bad or you want your life to mess up entirely, it's just a symptom of a deeper cause. Find the cause and you can cure the symptom.

When you're self-sabotaging:

• Figure out what the positive intention is of the self-sabotage – what are you trying to do *for* yourself?

• Retrain the part of you that is self-sabotaging to achieve the same thing a different way. E.g. to help you enjoy life by letting you live life.

• Find the real obstacle masquerading as self-sabotage.

• Take baby steps to find out exactly what is in your way.

• What else? What does your inner wisdom suggest you try?

Fear of being a tall poppy

I'm sure you've heard of tall poppy syndrome, where someone who stands tall, achieves something, stands out from the crowd is attacked, vilified, torn down, criticised. It's very common in the UK and in Australia – you see it all the time in the news media. One day successful singers, sports people, business people are lauded and celebrated, the next they are viciously torn down from their pedestal.

Because of this, we can hold ourselves back, shrink, not want to put ourselves out there for fear of, as one of my clients put it "putting my head above the parapet and getting shot at". It is entirely understandable, and sometimes, especially in cultures where tall poppy syndrome is widespread, it is not even conscious. It's a subtle fear, surreptitiously holding us back from being all we can be, as we see other people regularly being torn down for the crime of being human and fallible.

In the words of Taylor Swift "Haters gonna hate". This is going to happen. So remember this:

"It is not the critic who counts; not the man who points out how the strong man stumbles, or where the doer of deeds could have done them better. The credit belongs to

the man who is actually in the arena..." – Theodore Roosevelt

It is not those who tear down who matter. It is not those who criticise. It is those who try, who strive, and who put their all into something. This speech, by Theodore Roosevelt in 1910, is very inspiring in its entirety – google "The Man in the Arena"[3] and read it. Print it out, buy the poster and pin it to your wall, save it as your screensaver, and remember – you are the man or woman in the arena, covered in dust, even if you fail, daring greatly and possibly succeeding triumphantly.

That tall poppy syndrome exists is undeniable, but whether you will fall victim to it is debatable. Sure, there will be people who don't like what you do. That will be true no matter what you do in life. You're not here to please everyone. Which is lucky, because that would be impossible. You are here to be the best you that you can be, to follow those dreams that hide in your heart and stir your soul. So do. Shine anyway, even if you might get shot at when you put your head over the parapet.

Be the best you can be anyway, even if someone might criticise, mock or be jealous. Live the life you desire to live, even if someone might not like what you do. Get in that arena anyway and give life your best shot. Yes, it may hurt if people do criticise and take shots at you, but it will hurt less than if you diminish yourself out of fear, and live a life that stifles your spirit; full of regret and what if's.

Part of the problem here is putting people on pedestals, wanting them to be perfect because they're in the public eye or doing something different or rich or famous. Nobody is perfect, everyone makes mistakes, and if you put someone on a pedestal, at some point they will inevitably fall off. So don't put them on a pedestal. By all means love what they do, and admire their achievements, but don't expect them to be superwoman. No one is.

Humans are fallible, they make mistakes, they are human! So don't expect people to be paragons of virtue, you're setting them up for a fall. Including yourself. Don't expect yourself to be perfect, to have it all worked out, to be the expert...it's unrealistic, and actually people like vulnerability and authenticity. I remember the first time I had a coach who admitted to not being perfect in

---

[3] The speech was actually called "Citizens in a Republic", but this section on the Man in the Arena is more recognised now.

their business; it was a revelation. Instead of being the expert, they were a human - still learning, imperfect, and it was life-changing for me.

It made me realise what unrealistic and insane expectations I had of myself that were completely impossible to meet. We are so fortunate to live in the times we do, because we can get to know people behind the scenes a little and see what it's really like to build a business, write a book, live in paradise, make a dream come true. Find those people who are sharing the real story.

The story that includes failure, bad days, messy hair days, cockroach-in-the-shower-in-paradise days, days when the only writing that gets done is the shopping list, days when the delete button gets more wear than all the other keys put together. Real people, sharing their real lives. Not the phony marketing bullshit – find the real people, and surround yourself with those real people – online and in life.

Find those people who celebrate your first nasty comment on social media as a success milestone. Find those people who know how it feels to be a tall poppy and choose to grow anyway. Find those people who are in the arena, covered in dust, exhausted but triumphant. Find those people who will celebrate you sticking your head over the parapet with them, and will help to give you the armour to deal with the shots that (may) come your way. Find those people who can support and cheerlead your dreams and love you so much that you feel safe standing up as the tallest poppy in the field.

When you fear being a tall poppy:

- Read "The Man in the Arena", put it on your wall, save it as your screensaver.

- Shine anyway.

- Don't put people on pedestals, including yourself.

- Surround yourself with people who get it…both the fear and the desire to stand out anyway.

- What else? What does your inner wisdom suggest you try?

Not being able to see your brilliance

This is such a common obstacle for people. They just cannot see how amazing, how special, how magnificent, how incredible, how talented, how wonderful they truly are. Yes, I know you're tempted to skip over this section, because I can't be talking about you, because you're not amazing, special etc. NO! DON'T DO IT! Please read this chapter. Take it in, even if you don't think you are all of those wonderful things.

Open your mind to the idea that you might just be the most wonderful you that ever existed. Think about it for a moment, you are the only one of you there is. There are over 7 billion people in this world and you are the only you. You are a miracle of birth. Do you know all the things that had to happen for you to be born? It's wondrous! The ancestors that needed to connect, the spark of life that needed to be lit, the collection of cells it took to make a you.

You are unique and precious and one of a kind. No one else in the world has had the same experiences as you. No one else in the world has your unique blend of characteristics and gifts. You may not think you have gifts, but you do. You might be a great listener, brilliant with IT, a keen observer, witty and humorous, a fabulous baker, handy with DIY, a wonderful driver, an excellent gardener.

Many of us downplay our skills and talents precisely because they are so easy for us we don't see them as gifts. Look at your loved ones and friends, especially those who are self-deprecating and unable to see their genius. What do you see? Are they loving, patient, quick-witted, kind, thoughtful, helpful, funny, brave, clever, strong? What do you see that they don't see? Can you see their brilliance? I bet you can. So be open to the thought that just because you can't see your own brilliance, doesn't mean it's not there.

And that's a great way to tune into your own brilliance – see it in others. See other people's great qualities. See the uniqueness of them. See how their life has shaped them. See what they offer to the world. Feel free to praise it and celebrate it for them, to be their cheerleader, to help them see their brilliance. Just imagine if that person you love so deeply could see how wonderful they were. What might they be able to do and enjoy in their life?

Then ask your loved ones to do the same for you – to be a mirror for your magnificence. To be your cheerleader. To praise and celebrate what's great about you. To help you to see your brilliance. Be sure to choose carefully for this. That person who always points out your fashion faux-pas, the lippy on your teeth or where you messed up might not be the best cheerleader (although if they can turn that eagle-eyed criticism to praise, they'll be the best cheerleader you ever had).

Some of us are natural cheerleaders but cannot put up a shelf. Some of us are very handy at DIY but are unsuited to the task of cheerleading. It's a skill that takes time and practice to master. So you can either look for people who are naturals at it or train people up (or both, of course). While you're at it, train yourself up. Train yourself to be a great cheerleader.

Train yourself to notice your gifts, talents, unique skills and perspectives, and where you're just good at stuff. Sometimes looking at it as *brilliance* or *uniqueness* or *magnificence* can be off-putting, just too over the top. So start with what you do rather well. Start with what you're quite good at. Start with what you notice that's good about you. It could be little things, like that you keep your temper when you're itching to slap some fool at work. It could be that someone talked to you and you listened, it's rarer than you think!

It could be that you did your job well. It could be that you peeled the potatoes well, or put a lovely dinner on the table. Whenever you can, big up yourself, even if you don't feel like what you're doing is worth bigging up. Get some practice at bragging. Talk yourself up. Notice what you do that's good. Notice when someone compliments you and really take it in.

I have a compliment folder on my laptop, where I keep the nice things people have said about me and my work. So when I'm not seeing my brilliance, I can remind myself of the brilliance other people have seen and taken the time to share. These lovely compliments never fail to make me smile and raise my confidence in me.

Start to change the record from the constant litany about what you are doing badly to a catalogue of what you are doing well. Start to see how wonderful you are. Not for what you do or achieve or make happen, but just for being the one and only you. Be the model for your loved ones, and show them what it looks like to big up themselves rather than cutting themselves down.

When you're not seeing your brilliance:

- Be open to the idea that you are unique and special and wonderful.

- See the magnificence in others.

- Get your cheerleaders on the case.

- Start bigging yourself up…a lot.

- What else? What does your inner wisdom suggest you try?

Not trusting yourself

Do you fully trust yourself? Do you totally trust your intuition? Do you trust that even if everyone around you disagrees with your choices, you know what's right for you? A lot of people don't. Why would they?! We all have so much evidence of where we've messed up in the past – failed, got it wrong, made a fool of ourselves, had a disastrous relationship, done the worst job in the world, embarrassed ourselves and maybe even shamed our family.

Who on earth would trust *that*?

Wait! Stop right now. I just described *everybody's* life. No one gets through life without doing at least one of these things. I've done everything on that list but shame my family (at least I don't think I have). Everyone messes up somewhere. No one is perfect, although some people will pretend they are. I don't believe them, and I recommend you don't either. Give yourself a break. You're doing the best you can. Always.

I never used to trust myself at all…after all, I'd made so many mistakes. Then I realised that if I were to go back to the exact same situation, knowing only what I knew then, most of the time I'd have done the same thing all over again. Either because I didn't know better, or because I wasn't psychic and couldn't see disaster coming, or because I was optimistic that things would work out. I was doing the best I could at that time. So were you. I get to do better next time. So do you.

So be gentle on yourself with your past mistakes. In fact, work on letting them go. Most of us will remember our failures far more than our successes. I've had conversations with clients where they can remember a failure from a decade ago, but not a success from a week ago. Turn that around and start reminding yourself of what you did right, the good decisions you made, the relationship that worked for 10 years before it was time to move on, the great job you took, the times you made your family proud and excelled yourself.

And don't just focus on the big stuff – notice the small good decisions. Like when you ordered the perfect meal at a restaurant. No, it's not much, it's not a big deal, only it is when you're building up your trust in your self muscles. If you were trying to get someone else to trust in themselves, would you pick at and criticise every little thing they did, or would you find reasons to praise their good judgement and wisdom?

I rest my case.

We're all doing the best we can in life, and sometimes what we do makes more sense in hindsight than it did at the time. Like the client of mine who left a great job that she hated. Everyone around her thought she was crazy but she was unhappy in that job, and she knew she'd be better off out of there. Unemployment was far less stressful than the job.

Or the client who procrastinated writing her book for 2 years. At the time, she thought she was just a bad, lazy person, but then she realised that she needed more stability in her life than she had at that time. Once her home and family life fell into place, so did the writing. So even when you wonder why on earth you did something, trust that you had a good reason. Even if you can't see yet what that reason is. Because you're always doing your best. Trust in that.

By far the most powerful thing you can do to help yourself to trust yourself is to get out of your head and into your heart. Develop your intuition and get really comfortable with your inner wisdom. Inner wisdom sees the best in you. Inner wisdom knows you at your core. Inner wisdom knows all your secrets and foibles and failures, and still loves and trusts you. Inner wisdom is your connection to the divine, whatever that means to you.

To be honest, most of my failures and mess-ups have been a result of not listening to my intuition and inner wisdom. That disastrous relationship? Totally a result of not listening to my intuition. I didn't know better then. I do now. (But hey, sometimes I still don't listen, and that's ok too because not listening to my intuition reminds me how wise it is!) Get deeply in touch with yourself, and with the divine wisdom in you.

As you do, you'll find your inner knowing about what's right for you gets stronger, and your desire to please others, and to get answers from outside you will fade away. Because you'll trust, fully, that you and only you are the expert on your life, and that every failure is merely a learning experience without which you cannot succeed and be your best.

When you're not trusting yourself:

- Be gentle with yourself, you're doing the best you can. Always.

- Remember your successes, forget your failures.

- Remember we all have good reasons for what we do even if they don't seem to make any sense.

- Get really comfortable with your inner wisdom.

- What else? What does your inner wisdom suggest you try?

Imposter Syndrome (who am I to…)

Pretty much every Big Dreamer, creative or business person I have ever come across has experienced some form of imposter syndrome – that feeling of not being good enough, not knowing enough, of thinking 'who am I to do …' With stepping up into our best selves, with going for a Big Dream, with expansion and stretching out of our comfort zones comes some self-doubt. It's normal, it's natural, it's part of the process to shake it off and keep going anyway. Even Neil Armstrong (the first man on the moon) suffered from it[4].

Marianne Williamson sums this up beautifully in this quote:

"We ask ourselves, 'Who am I to be brilliant, gorgeous, talented, fabulous?' Actually, who are you not to be? You are a child of God. Your playing small does not serve the world. There is nothing enlightened about shrinking so that other people won't feel insecure around you."

Preach it, Marianne! I know that at first this feels quite confronting, scary, like a really big push onto an empty stage…at

---

[4] From Metro.co.uk May 2017 "Dealing with Impostor Syndrome: The secret to becoming a 'proper grown up' is realising that you will never actually be one"

.

least it did for me, and has for many of my clients over the years. Stay with it. Keep reading it. Consider it. Sit with it. Meditate on it. Let it sink in and soak into every fibre of your being. Pin it up on your wall. Make it your screensaver. Read it over and over again.

Who are you not to be the very best of you? Who are you not to share your gifts? Who are you not to fall in love with your life? Who are you not to go after those divinely inspired Big Dreams? Play big, go for it, be brave, be all that you can be. Of course, you've read enough of this book to know that I'm all about going for baby steps and gradual change. You don't have to leap out onto the world stage right this minute. Just begin to allow that what you have to say is worth hearing.

When I started writing I really struggled with this obstacle, thinking "who am I to write?", "I feel like a fraud", "I have no idea what I'm doing", "who am I to say this". I got over it (obviously). I did it anyway. Even though I felt like an imposter, even though I wasn't sure I was good enough, even though I wasn't sure I should be sharing my thoughts at all. I soon learned that my people like what I have to say.

In the DVD "You Can Heal Your Life" Louise Hay talks about the fact that all the speakers say broadly similar things, but that one speaker will say it in a way that you'll suddenly get it and it'll be like you never heard it before. You are unique and special and you have your own messages for the world. Whether that is through writing, or through your business, or just by living your best and most fabulous life – you have your own part of the jigsaw to complete.

There could be 1000 people out there doing something similar, but none of them can do it your way. The only person who can do you to perfection is you. So even though you may feel like an imposter, even though you may wonder who you are to do that thing, do it anyway. By doing it, you prove that you can, that you have something to share or say or do, and the more you do your thing, the easier it gets to do it without feeling like an imposter.

And remember, by being your best, shiniest, and most fabulous self, you're serving the world. You're sharing your heart, you're being fully you. There is nothing more valuable to the world. I can't even count the number of people who've inspired me just by doing what they do – writers, artists, singers, entrepreneurs; friends who simply live their lives the best way they can, and deal with their difficulties in such an inspiring way.

The more you can think about what you're giving to the world by doing what you do, the less you'll worry. Because it's not about you. It's about that one person who is going to love your book, or your painting, or is going to love buying from your business. It is about the people you will serve, you will help, you will inspire just by getting over your fear of being an imposter and going ahead and doing what you do.

You don't have to be writing masterpieces or healing the world, just by living full out, you're showing someone else what can be done. Just imagine if your daughter or your nephew or your best friend or your sister was inspired by you going after your dreams and loving life, and went and did the same thing. Wow, how powerful would that be if just by living your life and pushing through imposter syndrome, you helped someone else to go for their dreams too?

When you're suffering from imposter syndrome:

- Remember you are not alone in this. It's actually a really common obstacle!

- Remember Marianne Williamson's quote, who are you not to be the very best of you?

- Do it anyway, even though you feel like an imposter. You get confidence by doing. So do.

- Focus on what you're giving to the world

- What else? What does your inner wisdom suggest you try?

Feeling selfish

We're taught (often very early in life) that we should put others first – that to be a good person, we need to be totally selfless and not have needs at all. This is ludicrous, an archaic idea which has never worked in practice. Taking care of ourselves is an essential component in selflessness. If we are well cared for and feeling good we can pass this on to others (put your own oxygen mask on first, right?).

When we try to make everyone else happy, we end up making ourselves utterly miserable, and trust me when I tell you that the miserable martyr isn't that much fun to be around either. You deserve to enjoy your life too. You deserve to be able to follow your dreams too. You deserve to be selfish sometimes.

When you feel selfish for wanting to go for your dreams; when you feel selfish for needing time away from the roles you play in life (mother, father, daughter, son, employee); when you feel selfish for wanting a break from the relentless merry-go-round of being available for everybody 24/7; are you really being selfish or are you taking care of yourself?

When you are happy, and healthy, and feeling good, and having fun, and going for your dreams aren't you a better person to be around than if you're miserable, and exhausted, and stressed, and depressed, and feeling trapped in a life you don't want? When you are happy, this positively affects everyone around you.

So get selfish. You don't have to abandon your family and go jump on a flight to Barbados, just do something that you want to do; find a need you have and fill it, take some space and time just for you. You can explain if you want to – something like "hey, if I do this, I'm going to be happier, less snappy and easier to be around" but don't apologise for needing to be more than the roles you play in life.

Start to consider what you would love to do and find ways to fit that into your day. One of my clients loves music and loves to dance, and she discovered that food preparation time is a perfect time for loud music and unleashing her inner Beyoncé! Some days her family think she's crazy, other days they join in. However they react, she feels better and that's what's important.

People think that to take care of themselves is selfish, but actually there's nothing less selfish. If you fill yourself up, you have more to give than if you are constantly depleted, exhausted and worn down by life. As the saying goes – give from the saucer, not the cup. Fill yourself to overflowing, and give from the overflow rather than depleting yourself to give to others.

Sometimes that feeling of selfishness comes from not doing everything to perfection. You know, like the ads from the 50's of the perfect housewife who can cook and clean and support and nurture and still has great hair and wears a pretty dress. Maybe you have a more modern ideology of the woman with the career and perfect family (and great hair and perfect dress), the woman who has it all.

These ideals aren't real. Nobody's superwoman. Everyone's a mess to some extent in their lives. So quit trying to be superwoman all the time, stop trying to live up to an impossible ideal, and learn to accept help from others. Everyone can be selfish at times, and if you are doing everything for your loved ones, they'll probably let you do it. If you ask them for help, they'll probably do that too.

It's better to ask for help than to take it all on your shoulders for so long that you have a nervous breakdown or get sick. I've seen that happen to too many people who took care of everyone in their lives except themselves. Other people like helping, so let them. Even if they don't like it, ask anyway. They'll soon get used to it.

Now, I hesitated over putting in this last bit, because every client I've ever had who felt they were being selfish weren't really. However, this may help you to get your feeling of selfishness into perspective. Check the selfishness-ometer. How selfish are you really being, on a scale of 1-10 where one is you're a selfless angel and 10 is you're trampling on others to satisfy your own needs.

If you're known to be a harsh judge of yourself, get someone else to check the selfishness-ometer. If no one else is around to check with, imagine if someone you loved wanted to do the same as you do. Would you think they were being selfish? We often hold ourselves to higher standards than we would anyone else, so this exercise can help you to see that maybe you're being a bit hard on yourself.

It's also possible you will find you ARE being selfish! When that happens, either embrace it and claim your right to love your life, or consider whether you need to change the way you're doing things to be more considerate of others. Sometimes just a small change will give you what you need and allow you to give others what they need. Of course, the better you feel the more you have to give to others.

Actively hurting someone else with your selfishness is a very different thing to taking care of yourself and loving your life. Sometimes that line gets blurred, but often the people most worried about being selfish are the most selfless people (truly selfish people aren't that worried about being selfish). Find the balance between being a loving, kind, generous person (if that's who you want to be), and being strong and confident about your worthiness to live the life you want to live. No selfishness required, merely self-love.

When you're feeling selfish:

- Remember you deserve to enjoy life too (and that will have a positive impact on those around you).

- Embrace some selfishness…bit by bit.

- Stop trying to be superwoman and accept help.

- Check the selfishness-ometer.

- What else? What does your inner wisdom suggest you try?

Low confidence

So, here's something interesting I've learned about self-confident people versus under-confident people: they have the same thoughts. All people think "oh dear, I can't do that" or "I don't have the confidence to do x". The difference is entirely in what they do with those thoughts. Confident people brush off the under-confident thought and go do it anyway. Under-confident people believe the thought and stop. The majority of people lie somewhere between those two extremes.

But it's worth remembering that when you are low in confidence so is everyone else. To some extent everyone has the same under-confident thoughts. So it's not a deficiency in you. It's just something you can get better at - ignoring the under-confident thoughts and carrying on regardless. The easiest way to do that is just to take some action. Baby step action – small, easy steps that don't wake the sleeping lion of your fears.

The more baby steps you take, the more confident you will feel. The more baby steps you take, the easier it is to ignore the little voice saying "I can't do that because I am not confident enough" because you're doing it. Then start to ask what you would do if you had the confidence and start doing that - in baby steps. Act as if you were confident. If you were confident, how would you sit? What would you look like? What would you say to yourself? What body language would you show? Do it. Act confident.

Whatever you do, don't let your lack of confidence paralyse you. Under-confident isn't something you just are. It's something you may have learned. I was horribly shy and under-confident as a child. I got over it. Mostly. I'm still shy in some situations and under-confident at times. I'm working on it. You can too – just don't think you're stuck in under-confident land, you're not.

Have you seen the Sound of Music? Do you remember the song "I have confidence in me"?

"I have confidence in sunshine
I have confidence in rain
I have confidence that spring will come again
Besides which you see I have confidence in me"

If you know the film, you will know that this song comes in at a point when Maria does NOT have confidence in herself; she's out of her depth, scared and about to go into completely new territory. Rather than dwell on what she is unsure of, she concentrates on what she has confidence in, and works on building her confidence. In a pinch, what do you do? Build your confidence, or dwell on your uncertainties? Think about what you CAN have confidence in, or go into how you could cock it up?

The brave woman is not the one without fear (that's the idiot), but the one who carries on despite her fear. There are times when we aren't sure if we can do something. We have a choice whether we carry on regardless, or we choke and stay in the safe place. The trouble is, that safe place starts to become claustrophobic, erodes our confidence more and eventually hurts way more than carrying on regardless would have.

Have confidence in you and move forwards. I know sometimes that is far easier said than done, but you don't have to do it all alone. You can get the support of a friend, a teacher, a coach, a mentor. You can get support from someone who's been there, where you are. You can get support from Auntie Google. Google "raising confidence" and you'll find tons of resources to help you get confident. You don't need confidence to ask for help – you need the courage to be vulnerable and ask for what you need.

That can be super scary, but you can do it. You may be surprised. Whenever I've had the courage to be vulnerable and express my limitations, I have always been astonished at the number of people who say "me too". We think it's just us that have our foibles and fears and low confidence, but it's universal. It's part of being human – it's simply a case of learning to make your faith that you *can* do it stronger than your fear that you can't do it. I have confidence that you can do that.

When your confidence is low:

- Take action anyway, take some baby steps.

- Raise your confidence. Sit up straight, hold your head up high, smile and tell yourself you can do it. Because you can.

- Sing "I have confidence in me". I know that sounds a bit silly, but it really does help. If you detest that song, sing another one that you do like – Roar with Katy Perry, Try Again with Aaliyah, Be Brave with Sarah Bareilles (if you haven't watched the video for this, go watch it. I love the guy in the library!), get Stronger with Kanye.

- Get support. Get help. Get someone to give you a pep-talk, hold your hand, or even go with you.

- What else? What does your inner wisdom suggest you try?

Low self-worth and self-esteem

Much like low self-confidence, most people deal with a lack of worthiness or self-esteem at some point in their lives. Many of us wonder if we deserve better, deserve to have our dreams, and deserve to have the life we want. The simple answer is: yes you do. You are a slice of the divine. You deserve every good thing in your life. If you haven't had that up to now, it's not because you are not worthy of it.

We value babies for themselves. They don't have to *do* anything to be loved and valued and cherished and adored. They just are. This is what you deserve too. To be loved just because you are here. Not for what you do or what you've accomplished, but just because you are a special, precious, unique and wonderful human being. How much do you believe that? Assign a percentage to it. That's a good indicator of where your self-worth is at. If you have trouble believing it, your self-worth may be a little on the low side.

That's ok. It is what it is. You are where you are. Ready to change it? Don't worry. I'm not going to ask you to stand on a table in a crowded room and yell "I am worthy just because I exist. I am special and superb and sensational and you all are lucky to breathe my air"! Hey, if you want to do that, go for it, but there are easier ways to up your self-worth, to start to value yourself more.

For everything, but especially when your self-worth or self-confidence or self-esteem are low, think about just a 1% improvement. Don't try to go from 1% to 100% in one fell swoop – you're just setting yourself up for failure and making it hard for yourself. Don't do that to yourself. You deserve better. One of the easiest ways for you to give better to yourself is improving your self-care.

On a scale of 1-10, how cared for do you feel right now (by yourself), where one is "I don't" and 10 is "cradled in the arms of love"? Answer from your heart, not from what you think it should be. Answer honestly, don't pretend you're feeling cared for when you're not. The number doesn't matter much, it's just a benchmark. If your self-worth is low, your self-care is likely to be low too. So what can you do to feel more cared for right now? Do that and keep making self-care more of a priority in your life.

Next, work on your self-love. On a scale of 1-10, how loved do you feel (by yourself) right now, where one is "I don't" and 10 is "I adore myself"? Again, be honest. Again, the number is just a benchmark so don't use it as an excuse to beat yourself up. What can you do to love yourself more right now? Try finishing this sentence 10 times: "If I loved myself…" and go do one of those things.

Your self-worth and self-esteem will start to sneak up as you start caring for yourself and loving yourself more. The mistake we often make is to expect someone else's love and care to give us our worth and value. The trouble with that is that when that relationship ends, or if you're with someone who's just not great at mirroring your awesomeness, you're screwed! So this is totally an inside job.

Cheerleaders, lovers, friends, and family are fabulous and can help prop up our self-worth and self-esteem when we need it, but you need to be working on valuing yourself, loving yourself, treating yourself like the special, unique and precious being you are. Ironically, when we get good at this, other people tend to get better at it too (plus we have way less tolerance for people who are critical, rude or treat us badly).

Once your self-worth and self-esteem start to rise because you're treating yourself better, start asking yourself "if I deserved every good thing, what might change in my life?" You don't necessarily have to act on the answers, although you can if you want to. This is more an exercise in what if. What if you deserved every good thing? What if you could have what you wanted in your life? What if you were worthy of the best possible life?

You may find that you would change some relationships or circumstances. You may find you'd expect better from yourself, and from others – not in a demanding diva way, but in a high self-esteem, feeling you deserve good things way. You may find that you'd take more risks or try some new things. You may find that your dreams expand in ways you had never dared to imagine before.

Just let yourself entertain those thoughts, let yourself dream, let yourself consider what life could be like if you deserved all good things. At some point, it will sink in that you do deserve every good thing, and you'll have a blueprint for change. You won't need to burn your life down to the ground to change it – once your self-esteem rises, you'll start to see things change around you. The inside job will impact the outside world.

My last suggestion for dealing with low self-worth and self-esteem is another way to sneak up on it. Much advice for raising your self-worth is about learning to value yourself, which is great...but quite hard work when you have low self-worth. For me, and for many of my clients, sneaking up on it, doing the work behind the scenes without ever mentioning self-worth or self-esteem just works way better.

So learn to hear your inner wisdom. Get to know your inner self – especially your heart and soul, who have total unconditional love for you and can teach you by example not to be so hard on yourself, to be loving and kind and gentle with yourself. Your inner self will continually tell you that you can, you deserve, you are worthy. If it's not saying that, you're not connected to your inner self. Connect to the wisdom in you that knows you are unique and special and wonderful just by being alive, and you don't have to do a thing to deserve good in your life.

When your self-worth is low:

- Work on your self-care.

- Work on your self-love.

- Answer the question: "if I deserved every good thing, what might change in my life?"

- Get to know your inner self, connect to your inner wisdom.

- What else? What does your inner wisdom suggest you try?

Not believing in yourself or your dreams

To achieve anything in life, you have to believe in the possibility of it happening. Sports stars, actors, writers, mountain climbers, leaders, Big Dreamers...they all have to believe in the possibility of what they want happening. If they didn't believe in the possibility, they'd never start the journey, do the training, turn up to practice, take the next step, and keep showing up day after day after day.

"It's the possibility that keeps me going, not the guarantee." - Nicholas Sparks

You only need to believe in the *possibility*. You don't have to have 100% self-belief (although that can be helpful). You just have to believe enough to keep moving towards whatever you want. Honestly, you don't have to have as much self-belief as you'd think. I did not believe I could write a book. I wanted to; it was my deepest held dream, but I didn't believe I could.

But then, a chink of possibility opened. I started to wonder *what if I could*. I took a little action – wrote a few words, then a few chapters. The more action I took, the more my self-belief (and belief in that dream) built up until I had 100% self-belief that I could write as many books as I wanted to. Honestly, that level of self-belief came after the 2nd or 3rd book I wrote!! It took me a while to wrap my head around it.

We see the self-confident person who has 100% self-belief (think of sports people at the top of their games...Muhammed Ali or Usain Bolt for example), and that can be fabulous if you have that level of belief. Consider the possibility that they might have *worked on* that self-belief. What we see on the outside isn't what's going on inside. When we see someone achieving something great, they're at the end of that journey. What happened along the way is often unseen.

The times they faltered, the times they didn't believe, the times they doubted, the times they wondered if they would ever do it. Everyone has those times. If you work on your self-belief, if you work on your belief in your dreams, you can build up to 100% self-belief. There may be a person or two out there who had 100% self-belief from the get go, but I've never met one of them...most of us work up to it.

So how can you work on your self-belief? Check out the chapters on not being able to see your brilliance, low confidence and low self-worth and do all of those actions. Then make it your mission to tell yourself you are capable, you are brilliant and you can do it. This might feel odd at first, but you soon get used to it. Muhammed Ali told himself he was the greatest long before he actually was, and he grew into that greatness.

Imagine how you might act, what you might do if you believed in yourself fully and start behaving that way. You don't have to push yourself miles out of your comfort zone to do this... just lean against the edge of your comfort zone...whistling. (See the chapter on fear for more on this.)

I remember coming across the idea, years ago, that your dreams choose you as much as you choose them. If that's true, your dreams chose you knowing that you're the right person to follow them. So trust your dreams. Trust that your dreams have chosen a worthy host. Trust that there is adventure to be found in following those dreams. Trust your dreams to show you the way.

Trust that following that dream will bring the best out in you, that it will be fun and challenging and gloriously stretching for you (that's what dreams do for us). Trust that you can do it. Trust yourself. There is more to you than you realise. You are capable of more than you know now. Don't compare the start of your journey to the end of someone else's...they were most likely just the same as you at the start.

Following Big Dreams is an act of faith. We don't know what will happen when we start following our dreams. All we know is that the dream is calling. So we need to have faith. Have faith that things are working out for us, even when they look like they're not working. Have faith that there's a reason we have this dream. Have faith that we can do this. Have faith that our dreams chose us.

If you have faith in a higher power (God, Goddess, Angels, the Universe, Spirit, whatever you call it), call on that higher power, hand over your worries, ask for help to shore up your self-belief, ask for help to have faith. If you don't believe in such things, no matter. Ask your own higher self for the help, have faith in who you see in the mirror, and have faith that change is possible for you (you've changed since you were 14, right? So why not believe you can change again now?). Big Dreams are possible for you...believe!

When you are not believing in yourself or your dreams:

- Start with just believing in the possibility that you *could* do it.
- Work up to 100% self-belief.
- Trust your dreams and yourself.
- Have faith.
- What else? What does your inner wisdom suggest you try?

Worrying

"Confront obstacles as they appear, don't waste energy fearing what you may meet in the future." Isabelle Allende

This quote leapt out at me the first time I read The Kingdom of the Golden Dragon. I am a recovering worry-holic. I know it's a complete waste of time, as most of the things I worry about never happen. In fact, it's worse than a complete waste of time because worrying makes life worse. Worrying opens the door to fearfulness which can lead to bad decision making (which gives you more to worry about). Worrying can cause utter paralysis and stop you from moving forward.

Worrying is using your imagination to create things you don't want – horror stories for your life. Who wants that? And for most of your life, you've been dealing with what happens as it happens. You have had to, that's life. We confront failure, loss, uncertainty, bad outcomes all through life. We deal with them because we have to. I have no reason to doubt that you will continue to do so.

As I've got older, I have become more confident, more skilful, wiser, stronger, more optimistic, more positive, have more of a can-do attitude, I've learned to ask for help, and I take myself even less seriously. Taking all that into account, I could conclude that not only will I continue to overcome all obstacles I might meet in the future, I shall do it with wit, grace and flair. So will you.

"If a problem is fixable, then there is no need to worry. If it's not fixable, then there is no help in worrying." Dalai Lama

Of course, this is very easy for the Dalai Lama to say, not so easy for the worry-wart to do. So it may actually be easier to dive into the worry a little bit and find out what you're really concerned about. I find writing it out really helpful. Our worries tend to go in an endless loop, so if you actually write down what you're worrying about, you'll often find it's just the same thing over and over again. Then you can ask yourself:

Is there anything you can do about it? If so, do it and stop worrying.

If not, let the worries go. Again, sometimes easier said than done! So if you know there's nothing you can do and you keep going over and over it in your head, keep writing. Sometimes a solution presents itself; sometimes you just need that release of working through the possibilities and contingencies; sometimes you'll just realise that you're going round in an endless loop, and you need to go do something else to distract yourself.

By the way, you can also do this by talking, but be sure to pick the right person to talk to. A fellow worrier will not be helpful, most likely they will give you extra things to worry about. Someone who is the antithesis of a worrier will not help you either. Dismissing someone's concerns will not make them go away (even if they are ridiculous concerns). Find someone who is sensible, a good listener and has a good dollop of common sense.

If you've explored your worries and there's no solution to be had and you're still worrying, it's time for delegation and evasive action. If you're a believer, delegate to your higher power, your Guardian Angel, your Ancestors, your Guides. If you're not a believer, hand it over to your higher self. Then go distract yourself. If there's nothing you can do, carrying on worrying is not going to help the situation or you.

So go do something else – go for a walk, clean out a cupboard, dance your worries away, play a game you have to concentrate on, read a book, watch a film. One of my clients had spent days worrying about a situation they could do nothing about. To distract themselves, they played some card games, and during one game, came up with a great idea of what to do if what they were worrying about came to pass.

Hey presto! The worry was eased. Ironically, said excellent solution wasn't needed because the thing they were worrying about never came to pass! And isn't that most often the way?

"We suffer more often in imagination than in reality" – *Seneca*

The moon might hit you on the head. There is no point whatsoever in worrying about it. Don't let worry paralyse you – take your worries out, look at them, fix them if you can, let them go if you can't.

When you are worrying:

- Trust yourself to deal with whatever life throws at you when and if it happens.

- Write out your worries.

- If there's anything you can do about those concerns, do it.

- If not, let them go, hand them to a higher power, ask your guardian angel for help…and go back to #1…trust yourself to deal with whatever comes up.

- What else? What does your inner wisdom suggest you try?

'Outside' Influences

'Outside' Influences

We don't exist in a vacuum. There are so many things outside of our control that can happen to trip us up, stress us out and get in the way of the dreams we are trying to create. Remember that while things may happen to you that you have no control over, you do have control over how you react to them and how you deal with them. When things outside happen *to* you, you're helpless, but when you take charge of how you approach these outside events, you take back your power.

Like learning to dance in the rain instead of cursing your wet feet, learning to dance with outside influences will make life so much easier!

Life gets in the way

You know what it's like – there's so much to do, you're so very busy and important. Week after week after week you find you ran out of time to do anything with anything, and 3 weeks later you have zero recollection of what you were doing in all that very important busy work. How on earth can you make time for creating the life you want when life just seems to keep getting in your way?

But wait, the first thing you need to check is that you're not practicing some kind of avoidance strategy. "Life getting in the way" is another great disguise for other obstacles – and rather than see and deal with the real obstacle, we dodge it, get super busy doing not much and avoid our dreams for a while.

If you find that week after week *something* gets in the way but nothing memorable, then you need to sit down and work out what's going on. Are you avoiding working on your dreams? (You know yourself well, you'll know if you're avoiding, even just a little bit.) If so, what's the real obstacle? Why are you putting life in the way? When you find the real obstacles underneath life getting in the way, go check out those chapters.

And if you find that you have been avoiding, and putting life in the way, please don't beat yourself up – *it is what it is*. Once you can see what's really going on, you can deal with it. There's usually a positive intention behind our avoidance strategies – we want to avoid fear or failure, we don't want to take on too much, we're protecting ourselves from disappointment, we're believing old scripts that people like us don't have dreams come true.

So be kind to yourself. Beating yourself up over something like this is totally counter-productive. I had a client who had created a bad association with her dream, because every time she thought about it, she gave herself a hard time about not having done anything with it. So she started to associate the dream with getting criticism from herself. Who would want to spend time on their vision when it means stress and self-criticism?! Not me.

Be curious, get out your magnifying glass and your Inspector Clouseau hat, find the clues and when you do, shout "aha!", and sort out whatever the problem is. No self-criticism is required.

So you've found some reasons that life's been getting in the way, maybe some other obstacles that were dressing up as life getting in the way, perhaps an excuse or three. Now it's time to make a decision. Is your vision for your life important enough for you to rearrange your life to accommodate it? Like you have to do when you go from single to coupled-up, or from having no kids to being a parent?

It's your choice. You get to choose whether you spend another 5 years letting life get in the way (when nothing much is actually happening, rather than a seismic change in life – that's a different obstacle altogether, and I talk about this in the next chapter) or whether you change something. You get to choose to keep living the way you have been or to adjust and make space for what you want to create.

Once you've made the decision to make working on creating the life you want a priority, book in that time. Behave as if this was deeply important to you (it is, right?) and find the space and time for it. It's easy to say "when I have time" or "at the weekend" or "next week" or "when I've retired in 50 years' time" but why wait that long? Also, when you're that vague about the when, it's really easy to forget.

I know that I want to spend more time with my friends, but if we say "let's get together soon", months and years pass before we catch up. When we put a date in the diary, we meet up. It's as simple as that. So put the time in your diary. You've decided to make your dreams a priority, now decide when they will get your time. Please don't complicate this by deciding you need 80 hours of clear time...that never happens!

Do what you can with the time you have and a funny thing will happen; when you make time for your dreams, time expands.

One of my clients decided her train commute time would be her time for planning her Big Dreams, and taking what action she could. Within weeks, she had also ditched the lunchtime gossip-fests with colleagues 2 or 3 days a week, and stopped watching a soap opera she wasn't that interested in.

She went from life getting in the way all the time to working on her dreams for 8+ hours every week without feeling as if she'd lost anything. It's amazing what happens when you make a decision and back it up with some time, space and action. Life will get in the way sometimes, it's the nature of life, but when it's happening all the time and you don't know where your days are going, it's time to take the reins and lead life where you want to go.

When life gets in the way:

- Check whether life is getting in the way or you're avoiding – is life getting in the way another obstacle in disguise?

- Don't beat yourself up over it, it happens to us all.

- Make the decision to make your dreams a priority.

- Book in the time to work on your vision for your life.

- What else? What does your inner wisdom suggest you try?

A personal earthquake or seismic change in your life

Sometimes life throws a grenade into your world, causing everything to shift and change. Something happens that stops you in your tracks, distracts you, takes up all your time and attention, and all the work you've done on your dreams sits in a corner gathering dust. It happens to us all. Life is unpredictable and full of surprises, some good, some God-awful. It could be a new job or new child or an amazing inheritance. Or it could be illness in you or a family member, a loss, a disaster that rocks your world.

Be gentle with yourself, rearrange your life to deal with the disruption as much as you can, take great care of you if it's a stressful change; and do the best you can with what you have.

When shit happens, you do what you've got to do. If you have a mom in hospital and sick kids and 3 jobs and a hubby working away, this is perhaps the time to focus on taking care of you so you can juggle the mayhem of life.

Once things settle, or you start to get into a routine, you can get back to your dreams. I know you may not want to hear that, but you've only got so many resources available to you, and trying to do it all will wear you out. Sometimes you just need to give yourself permission to press pause. I know when I've had loved ones in hospital, or lost family members, I didn't have the bandwidth for Big Dreams, I was just trying to get through each day with my sanity intact.

When I was in those situations, sometimes I tried to keep going and it was a waste of time. I didn't have the capacity for it, the energy for it or the mental and emotional ability to do it. So it was a kindness to myself to allow myself to let it go. Just for a little while. Not forever. Just until the crisis was past, or the grief lessened and I had room in my brain and my heart for more than sadness.

Be patient and take great care of yourself. If you're in an unusual or crisis situation, it will pass, but until it does, breathe deeply and be patient. And make sure your self-care is excellent – you need to be at the top of your game when life gets mad. Depending on what exactly is getting in the way, you may be able to just scale back a bit and keep the engine running on your dreams.

I had a client whose mom was in hospital, so on the drive to visit her she listened to inspiring audios, and if her mom was asleep while she was there, she'd whip out her notebook and make notes of what she'd do when she had the time. She also started to accept help from friends and neighbours so that she could keep her business going while also visiting mom, taking care of her family, and working full time.

Which brings me to possibly the most important thing to do when life hits you with a seismic shift: get help and support. Just as you would hate it if your friends struggled on alone, they don't want you to put on a brave face and wear your underwear over your trousers. They want to help you. Let them. Give up any ideas of being superwoman and let someone cook for you, or take the kids, or get a bit of shopping for you.

Often when life turns upside down, the smallest kindness can make the biggest difference. Learn to receive with grace when you need a bit of help and let other people enjoy being generous and kind. Just don't expect them to guess what you need – they may think what you most need is a shoulder to cry on when actually someone taking care of your laundry would be the best thing in the world. So tell people what they can do to help.

At some point, the disruption will cease, ease, or it will become your new normal and you can get back to the dreams you were chasing. Be sure you're ready. If you've had a truly earth-shattering interruption, it may take some time for the dust to settle. Also, take the time to check back in with what you want. It's amazing what clarity comes from a seismic change in life.

When I lost a close family member, many of the things I had thought were important to me just dropped away, making my vision for my life and business a lot simpler. So take the time to re-clarify your vision. Then get back to taking action…perhaps at a slower pace, perhaps with greater wisdom, perhaps with deeper perspective, perhaps with a new drive or direction.

Seismic shifts often bring to the surface new dreams and new ways of being. They demand that we pause our dreams, and this can act as a filter, getting rid of old patterns and ways of being. So be sure to let the dust settle and reassess what you want from your life before continuing on your old paths. You may find the horizon has expanded and something new is calling.

When life gets in the way:

- Be gentle with yourself, take care of you and allow yourself to press pause if that's what you most need.

- Accept help. Delegate. Drop things that don't need to be done by you. People love helping, so let them help.

- Keep the engine running if you can. If not, accept you'll get back to your dreams when the earth stops shaking.

- When you're ready, check in with yourself and your dreams and then get into action again.

- What else? What does your inner wisdom suggest you try?

No money

This is another obstacle that is so common it's almost a cliché. For many of my clients, it's their go to obstacle – the first thing that gets in the way of anything and everything they want. So because they need the money and they don't have it, that's the end of their dreams. Only it's not – there's always a way forward from this obstacle. So if you find that lack of money is an obstacle for you, don't panic, because it's easier than you think to get over this obstacle.

If what you need is money, you can make money. You probably have been for years, in many different ways. You have probably found money at some point in your life. You have probably been given money at some stage. Unfortunately, you've also probably had experience of money being scarce, which makes people fear money and think it's really hard to get. I understand that – I've been there myself. I've had to train myself to be creative when I come up against the obstacle of no money.

The first thing to do when you are stuck on the *no money* obstacle is to get clear on exactly how much you need. I've lost count of the number of times a client has said "I don't have the money" and when asked how much they need, they don't know. If you don't know how much something actually costs, how can you know you don't have that amount?

Once you find out how much you need, start saving it now. Even if you think it will take you 5 years to save *enough*, start saving now. Savings magically attract other savings (but if they don't seem to straight away, don't worry about it - just keep saving anyway). One of my clients needed to save £1000 but could only save £5 a week…but she kept saving, and soon found she could put more aside. Not only that, but she got what she needed for less than she expected to pay. It's magical when you commit to saving for something.

You may also find that the "money" obstacle is a smoke-screen for the real problem. For example, I wanted some work doing – I didn't think I had enough money but when I investigated how much it would cost, it turned out I had the money. But then I found myself resisting delegating the task, because I'm a control freak. I'm working on that!

Clients often find if they had the money, there'd be something else getting in the way. So check…what might money be a smokescreen for? If you had the money, would you go ahead and do whatever it is you want to do? Or is there something else that might get in the way? It's worth diving deep on this; you don't want to spend 6 years saving the money for something only to find you don't want it after all.

Once you're sure it's the right thing for you, and you're committed to saving for it, check your facts. Do you really need that much? Can you bootstrap it? Can you do it a different way? If you want to go to Necker Island (and you don't have a spare £280,000), can you go to another Caribbean island for a fraction of the cost? Or meet other businessmen in your area for the cost of a networking meeting?

Get your creative hat on. What do you really want and how can you achieve the same end in a different way for less money? For example: couch-surf to travel the world, create a free website instead of getting a fancy-schmancy one, or shop around. Find more cost-effective ways to do the same things (or similar enough), bring back bartering and trade your skills for other skills (or for some cash to go towards what you want).

On that very subject, it's time to break the belief that money is impossible to get. Make a list of 50 things you could do to make money – be creative, have fun with it, and write down all your ideas; even if you know you won't do them, they'll only make pence, or you think they're silly. Every time I do this exercise, I put "drive a taxi"...something I have no intention of doing, but the idea is always there.

This is a fun exercise to do once in a while even when you aren't trying to save for something specific; it helps you to realise that money is easier to get, and you have more options than you think. One of my clients sold all the junk from her attic and raised enough for a holiday, a VIP session with me, and a deposit on a new car. There are literally thousands of ways to legitimately get your hands on money.

Once you have made your list, do one of those things. Even if it's a miniscule amount towards what you need, income attracts more income and entrepreneurial thoughts attract other entrepreneurial thoughts.

Money is eminently gettable. You just have to be creative, open to receiving and relaxed about it – if you're stressed and grasping, money runs like water through your fingers. The more you play with it, have fun with it, be inventive, and stay unattached, the easier it is to get money. Being unattached simply means that if it works, great; if not, you tried, and you learned something. It's all good. When it comes to money, the more relaxed you can be about it, the better.

When you've got no money:

- How much do you actually need? Get super specific about what you need, and start saving now.

- If you had the money, would you do what you want to do or would there be another obstacle in your way? Is money just a smoke-screen?

- Get creative – is there another, bootstrappy way you can do the same thing?

- Take the cash out of the attic – what can you sell? How can you make some money?

- What else? What does your inner wisdom suggest you try?

No time

Oh boy, if I had a pound for every time I heard this one, I wouldn't need to work ever again. So, the first thing you need to know is that this is a really common obstacle – many people say that lack of time gets in the way of them making their biggest visions for their life a reality. We're all time deprived these days. We fill every spare minute with doing, so of course we have no time left-over.

You have to make a conscious choice about where you spend your time. We've all got the same number of days in a week, hours in a day, and minutes in an hour. How much of that time you can devote to creating your life is dependent on what you do to earn money, on family, on the length of your commute and so on, but it's entirely your choice how you spend that free time. Yep, I know, it's easy for me to say, but trust me, everyone has to make the choice to make their Dreams important enough to give them the time they need.

When this takes time away from family, it can be a tough choice to make. It's still a choice though, and you can re-make it every day. You can choose to take the time you need for you one day. Another day you can choose to take care of your sick child, because that's your priority. It's not a choice between your dreams and your family, it's a choice as to what's going to make you and your family happiest.

But when you're running frantically through life, crying "I'm late, I'm late, I'm late!" like the white rabbit from Alice in Wonderland, it's hard to see how you can make any other choices as to what to do with your time. It's practically impossible to make good choices from a position of stress and frenzy. So first, you need to slow down.

Yeah, I know you don't want to. You want to speed up and fill more spare moments with doing. It won't work. You'll burn out and although multi-tasking is seen as effective and positive, it's not. It frazzles our brains, stresses us out and means we can't see the wood for the trees that are flashing by at high speed.

So slow down. Take space. Breathe. Pause. (The more those words stress you out, the more you need this prescription.) Meditate. Stare at the sky. Allow your brain to rest. Relax. However you can. I had a client who set a timer on her phone for 30 seconds and forced herself to sit still and do nothing for those 30 seconds. Another sat in the car for exactly one song before going to and leaving work. Another meditated for 5 minutes every morning at the start of work and every evening when getting home.

Whatever way of slowing down appeals to you, do it. You don't have to be on a go slow for the rest of your life (although you might want to). You just need to be able to sit back long enough to see what can be juggled, what can be delegated, and what can be dropped in order to give yourself the time you need.

Often there are compromises that can be made: Daddy time on Saturday mornings, Grandparent weekends, dropping old habitual appointments that no longer serve you, using your lunch hour for something other than bitching about work, reclaiming your commute time to do something positive.

For example, I've had clients who read inspirational books, journal or meditate on the train. I've had clients who use their drive to work to listen to inspirational audios, have car discos (safely, of course) to up their feel-good vibe, and dictate into their voice notes app to do's, ideas and even chapters for books.

Most of us never take the time to stop and see what we are doing in our frantic busy time. We're too busy. Ironic, right? But when you do, you'll often find that something you thought was a non-negotiable is actually something you don't like doing and can drop. Look at what you're choosing to make more important than your dreams. Ironing, chores, surfing the internet, shit TV?

Outsource the ironing, get help with the chores, set a time limit on your surfing time, and switch off the TV. Suddenly you have more time. One client discovered that outsourcing her ironing would cost £20 for work that would have taken her 3 hours. Another found her husband could use the vacuum cleaner with a bit of training (it's not that hard). Another realised that she spent over 20 hours a week on the internet or watching programs she wasn't interested in.

I don't want you to throw out your telly – I love TV and watch a lot of it myself. Nevertheless, if I need more time it's the first thing to go, because it's not that important to me. By hook or by crook you need to find little pockets of time where you can work on the things that are most important to you – even just 5 minutes here and there to start with. So often, we don't do what we can with what we have (5 minutes here and there) because it's not enough, but it is better than nothing.

1 hour a week on your dream life in 10 minute increments isn't enough, but it's better than no minutes at all. Over time, those small increments of time add up. Before you know it, you've spent 50 hours on writing your book or building your business or loving your life. Plus, once you're already taking time for the life you want, you'll find it easier to find more time because it's fun, and momentum breeds momentum.

No time is just an excuse – you need to make and take the time you need. No one will give it to you. You have to take control of your life and figure out how you can do what you want to do. Gently, curiously, openly. If you absolutely *had to* find 3 hours in your week, how would you do it? I know you can, and if you choose to make your dreams more important than your busyness you will.

And if you are genuinely without any spare time right now (I've never met anyone who can't find any time, but that doesn't mean you don't exist), start to plan for how and when you will make time in the future. For example, 3 children under 5 leave very little spare time, but over the next few years, more time will be freed up – plan ahead for when they're all in nursery or school. What will you do then? If you don't plan it, you'll find the time filled with busywork. Claim your time back as soon as you can.

When you've got no time:

- SLOW DOWN.

- Once you are calm, look at what can be juggled, delegated and dropped to make room for the things you want to do.

- Look at where you are currently using your time – what is more important than your vision? Chores, TV, uncle YouTube and cousin Facebook?

- Find small blocks of time in your week to work on your most important goal or vision – these can be *just* 5 minutes if you are super busy – take and make time for your most important priorities, even if it is just a small amount of time.

- What else? What does your inner wisdom suggest you try?

Energy and health issues

There are times in most of our lives when our health and energy become a problem – to the point that it gets in the way of us having the most magnificent life possible. Those damn bodies of ours, right? Er, no. Listen, your body is the machine that gets it all done, so taking care of it is always your highest priority (plus your mental, emotional and spiritual health), because if you have poor health and no energy, it is incredibly difficult to do anything.

So, the first thing you must do when you have energy and health issues is *listen* to your body. Listen to the messages you're being sent, and start to take excellent care of yourself. In my late 20's I was diagnosed with Chronic Fatigue Syndrome, which later turned out to be MS, but the consequences were exactly the same. I had days when I was so exhausted, I couldn't get out of bed.

Having CFS/MS forced me to start taking care of myself: body, mind, heart and soul. It forced me to listen to the messages of my body. I discovered I couldn't burn the candle at both ends and in the middle. What I learned from that experience has stood me in good stead for the past 15 years: if I don't listen to my body's whispers, it will shout. And if I still don't listen, I'll be incapacitated.

I know that when you're going through it, the illness or lack of energy is a pain in the arse, getting in the way of you living the life you want to lead. Unfortunately, the more you resist, the more you delay your recovery. In some cases, you make yourself a lot worse. So when you're having energy or health issues, take notice of them. Listen to your body. Learn to give yourself the best care possible.

Even if you feel restricted by it. Even if you really want to just carry on as if your body isn't worn out. Been there, done that. I know with certainty that it just doesn't work (I experimented extensively over 3-4 years with ignoring the symptoms, trying to get back to normal too soon and doing too much. It never worked).

Pay attention to your inner knowing, learn what your body needs to thrive. Your health or energy issues are telling you something...what is it? Once we get to the point of being ill or exhausted, we've often been busy ignoring our body's messages for years. The illness or energy issue is telling you to stop doing that and to start listening.

Make sure you get help to take care of you. From everywhere and everyone you can – friends, family, doctors, alternative practitioners, other people who have what you have. Depending on your health issues, this might not be easy. In my case, it was Auntie Google who helped – doctors could do nothing for CFS in the 90's. I found websites and communities who were talking about fatigue and sharing their experiences.

Just knowing that I wasn't alone in dealing with extreme fatigue helped, and a lot of their advice was very helpful. I also learned another important lesson – just because the medical establishment has no idea what to do, that doesn't mean there is nothing to be done. Alternative and complimentary therapies are really helpful for CFS and MS (as well as many other illnesses and conditions), as are lifestyle changes.

Which brings me nicely to the next point: make the lifestyle changes you need to make to keep yourself healthy and energised. I didn't want to. I wanted to carry on living life to the fullest – drinking, dancing, and getting in at 7am on a weekend. That lifestyle was making me ill. It took 3 years for me to realise I just couldn't do it anymore. Sometimes those lifestyle changes will be temporary, but sometimes it's a forever change and you will need to choose: do you want to be healthy and energised or keep abusing your body and feeling like crap?

Ultimately, health and energy challenges are asking us to pay attention to our bodies, to learn to take better care of ourselves. Since learning this myself, I have become a pulpit-basher for self-care. Most of us only give ourselves the bare minimum of care –

just enough to keep us going. It's not enough. When you take better care of your car than you do yourself, it's time to learn magnificent self-care.

Treat yourself as the most precious item in your life. You are. So be really gentle with yourself and honour your body's messages. Pay attention to your persistent health issues (headaches, insomnia, catching every cold going) and find their root cause to heal them, instead of masking the problem with medication. Hear the often very unsubtle messages your body, mind, heart and soul are giving you, and respond to them with action that nurtures you.

In the face of many of the other obstacles, I'll tell you to just keep taking action, but not this one. With this one, make your health your highest priority. You can't just replace your body when it wears out, so it's important that you get yourself in the best condition possible. Once you are feeling better, or once you're managing your symptoms, then you will want to get back to your Big Dreams and make 'em happen. But first, give your body the attention and care it needs.

When you have energy/health issues:

• What are your energy/health-issues trying to tell you? Listen to them.

• Get help – from wherever you can – doctors, alternative practitioners, Auntie Google, friends and family.

• Make the changes you need to make.

• Learn, and practice magnificent self-care[5].

• What else? What does your inner wisdom suggest you try?

---

[5] The next book I will be working on (to come out in 2018) will be a book about self-care, so if you want to learn more about this, look out for that book. If you need it earlier than 2018, get in touch and I'll put you on the list to be a beta reader.

Other People

So, I guess that you, like me, KNOW that if only the world would do as you tell it to, it would be a perfect place, right? If other people would just behave the way you think they should, your life would be perfect. However, those pesky other people think the same thing. If only you'd behave in a way that is acceptable to them, their life would be perfect. I suspect, like me, you have no intention of living your one and only life according to someone else's rules. So why on earth would you expect them to live by your rules?

Let other people be who they are, don't try and make them be how you think they should be. They won't. It's a waste of precious energy. All the time you spend in their business, you're not in your own business. Get your own house in order. Ironically, people often do change when you stop trying to force the issue, but don't expect that. Simply work on yourself and leave them alone.

"Do not seek to straighten another. Do a harder thing instead. Straighten yourself" - Buddha, teachings on relationships

This can be so difficult when we're talking about people who are close to you, loved ones whose opinions are important to you, or people who can put a spanner in the works of your dreams. Other people's reactions often say more about them than they do about you. Be compassionate, understanding and supportive. If you've just said "I want to move our family to Mars tomorrow", it might be a lot for them to deal with. Be aware that what you do does impact others, and might scare them or irritate them.

You don't have to tread on eggshells and people-please to try to keep them happy, but sometimes a bit of thoughtfulness goes a long way. As does trying to find solutions that work for everyone, not compromises that leave everyone a bit pissed off. This means a bit of effort on everyone's part to find those solutions, but its well worth getting into that habit. While you're seeking the solution that works for everyone, you continue doing what you can towards your vision.

Your loved ones might not understand your dreams (this happens often with parents). This is your life, it's your journey, and it's your vision for your life. Other people will get on board, or not. Your job is to stay in your own business and keep going. I know this can be easier said than done when a loved one is unsupportive, or even actively sabotaging your efforts but see them as just another obstacle to navigate – you can work around them if necessary. You never know, their contrariness might just be the thing that sets you on a new, and even better path.

It can be crazy-making when the people you most love aren't the people who support you most, but maybe that's just not their sphere of genius. They may give the most excellent hugs, they may be extremely practical, they may have tech know-how, but not the skill of cheerleading. That's ok – let them be awesome at what they're awesome at, and get someone else to do the bits they're not so good at.

Find supportive people, find people who get what you're doing, and surround yourself with a Dream Team. You get to choose who gets on that dream team, and who stays off it. If you really want to get your loved ones on board, train them up a bit. Clear requests are a great place to start.

I had a client whose husband constantly knocked all her ideas, but when she told him she wanted him to believe in her, he was astonished. "I do," he said. "I just want to help you by pointing out all the pitfalls you will face." She didn't realise this was his idea of supportive, and he didn't realise that naysaying wasn't her idea of supportive.

Don't expect other people to guess what you want and need from them. Yes, it would be great if they were all psychic and knew what you were thinking…WAIT! Perhaps that wouldn't be such a good thing. Anyway, most people aren't psychic. A lot of them aren't that emotionally attuned to the needs and wants of others. So educate them (nicely). Tell them what you want them to do.

Also, consider using "outcome focused communication". Think about what you want when you start communicating, and consider the best way to achieve that end. Starting the conversation with "you're a jackass" when you want more loving time with your partner isn't necessarily the best way to get what you want. Be aware of how you're communicating what you want and need – is it working? Get pragmatic. Do what works with your loved ones.

I've talked here about the influence of loved ones. I know that it can be all sorts of people who create enormous obstacles in your journey to a fabulous life, but you can choose how much those obstacles stop you or whether you just say, in the words of Coco Chanel:

"I don't care what you think of me. I don't think about you at all."

It's your life, you get to live it your way, and the faster you can disentangle yourself from the need for approval from people whose approval you don't need, the better.

When other people are getting in the way of your dreams:

- Don't try to change other people – it's a waste of energy.

- Give some thought to solutions that leave everyone happy – not compromises, but creative solutions.

- Get support from supportive people.

- Be clear about what you want from your people. Don't expect them to guess what you want.

- What else? What does your inner wisdom suggest you try?

Comparison-itis

Good old comparison-itis. Looking at someone else, seeing them being magnificent and shrinking yourself in comparison. What a wonderful way to trip ourselves up and make ourselves feel really bad about life. The problem is that comparison is a lie – we can only see the outside of someone else, we can only see their public face, what they're happy to show to the world or what they put on the internet.

We cannot see the full story. We cannot see what is going behind the scenes, only what is put on the stage. We're comparing that to the inside of us – with everything we know about ourselves, our struggles, our faults, our failures. It's not a fair comparison. This comparison shows you nothing about what you're capable of. This is my favourite quote about comparison:

"Comparing an apple and an orange leaves both apple and orange feeling inadequate" - Anon

The only thing the two have in common is that they're fruit. That's it. They have their own wonderful characteristics and taste and colour, they're not designed to be each other. You are not designed to be someone else. You are you, with your own wonderful characteristics and tastes and colours and destiny. Keep your focus on yourself. By all means learn from other people, be inspired by other people, but never let what other people are doing discourage you from walking your own path.

Instead, use others as fuel for your path. If they can, you can. Once Roger Bannister broke the 4-minute mile in 1954 (once thought to be impossible), it opened the possibility up to other athletes, and many have now done it. So when you see someone else doing or having or being what you want, take it as encouragement that you can do it too; be inspired by them.

Thanks to the wonders of modern technology, we can now find out more about others than ever before. Through social media and blogs we can pick up all sorts of success tips from others. So find the people doing what you want to do and find out what they're doing that you can use. I'm not talking about copying them, plagiarising them or becoming their clone, but looking at what they're doing or have done to get where they are, and learning from them.

For example, one of my clients was comparing herself to a friend who appeared to be enjoying her life so much more. When we broke down what this friend was doing, she was optimistic, generally positive, didn't whine about work (despite hating her job) and she did things regularly that she enjoyed. All things my client could take on to help her enjoy life more.

Once you've learned what you can from others, get back in your own business. I remember seeing an Olympic rower being interviewed before the Olympics: they were asked about the other teams, the weather, and so on. For everything outside their direct control, they answered "not in my boat". They were only interested in what was happening in their boat – anything outside was nothing to do with them. Especially any comparison with other athletes.

There is nothing you can do about someone else, so why think about it? I love the complete focus of Olympic Athletes. You can learn so much from them about mind-set…even if you have no intention of taking up an Olympic sport. When you are comparing yourself to someone else, you are putting your attention on something outside your boat. This won't help you make your life the best it can be. Your attention needs to be inside your boat – on your life, on your gifts and experience, on your qualities and resources.

Comparison with anyone else drags you down, makes you feel bad and slows your journey down. I know, I do it, and it's never a positive force. So don't do it to yourself. It's a habit you've got into…stop it. Whenever you notice the script of "she's so much better/prettier/younger/ cooler/shinier/richer/more whatever than me", stop. Interrupt the pattern, wish her well and go do something else.

Remind yourself that apples and oranges cannot be compared. Remind yourself to be inspired, not deflated by the light of others, and let other people become fuel for your dreams instead of brakes.

When you're comparing yourself with others:

• Remember you are comparing what you know about you (everything) with what you know about them (not a lot).

• If they can do it, you can too. Be inspired by others rather than discouraged.

• When you find people you admire, look for things they do that you can use to help your life.

• Take your attention off them and put it back on your dreams for your life. Put your attention in your own boat.

• What else? What does your inner wisdom suggest you try?

Leaving people behind/changing

When you start creating a life you deeply love, you may find yourself changing, growing, expanding, and leaving other people behind. This sense of separation (whether it's true or not) can be painful and uncomfortable, but it's actually quite natural. We tend to make a bigger deal out of it when it happens because we are changing rather than because of other life shifts, like leaving school or changing jobs.

But think about it – are you still in touch with all your school friends? Maybe you even changed friends while still at school. Are you still in touch with everyone from your first job? Are you still in touch with the people you lived next door to in your twenties? Life evolves and shifts, and we tend to evolve and shift with it. We lose touch with people. Maybe people we still love and would love to spend time with, but they live on the other side of the world.

As our lives change, our interests change and often our friendships change too. If you were a party girl before you became a mom and you became sensible while other friends carried on going out and getting wasted, chances are you lost touch with those people for a time. Sometimes you come back together later when life shifts again, but sometimes the friendship becomes more of a reminiscence than a close connection.

Becoming a mom, taking on a more responsible role at work, travelling the world, going away to college, doing things differently, all change you as a person. Sometimes old friends can't, or won't, catch up with who you are now (like the friend who still invites me out for a piss-up on the town when I haven't been a drinker for nearly 15 years). C'est la vie.

I don't mean to diminish the pain of leaving people behind at all, because that estrangement is painful. It is also natural, and it makes those friendships that do survive the test of time and transformation even more precious. I have friends I have known since I was a small child, and our friendship has survived all the things we've done and been through. There are others I think of often and still love, but I just don't see anymore.

So the next time you find yourself feeling that the changes you're making in your life are distancing you from people you love, be gentle with you. In my experience, staying the same isn't an option.

"And the day came when the risk to remain tight in a bud was more painful than the risk it took to blossom." – Anais Nin.

When we're creating our best lives, we can't stay the same just to prevent someone else feeling uncomfortable or confronted.

Allow yourself to be where you are, to go where you're going, and to mourn what seems to be changing (it may be temporary, you never know), and be gentle with the people you are leaving behind too. It can be really challenging and difficult when someone who was your constant companion changes, moves, and starts to become someone different. Allow your friends to be where they are.

Let it be ok that they think you're crazy, or that they're not interested in your life-changing new ideas, or that they are happy to be in the job that has you bouncing off the walls. Let it be ok that they don't understand what you're up to. Let it be ok that they want you to stay the same...they call it a comfort zone for a reason, it's comfortable. Let it be ok that they don't want to come with you, backpack in hand, to deepest darkest Peru, or wherever you are going.

And at the same time, do involve them. I went through a little phase of "no one takes an interest in my business". Know why? Because when they asked me about it, I would say "it's alright" and change the subject! Face palm. No wonder they took no interest, I made it sound tedious beyond belief and shut them out. My reasoning was that they wouldn't get it, especially if I was working on something quite woo-woo, but I never gave them the chance to get it or encouraged them to take an interest.

Once I did trust them with what I was up to, they were more interested and engaged and it turned out that my assumptions were (mostly) wrong...they do get it. Unless I talk about the technology behind ebook creation or podcasting, then I tend to see their eyes glaze over. That just makes those who do understand the techy conversations all the more precious.

As well as sharing more of the new you with them, find new things to do together. So for example, I used to be a big drinker and all my friendships involved alcohol in copious amounts. When I stopped drinking, pubs and clubs became less attractive to me, so I had to find other fun things to do. One of my tequila-drinking buddies became my Shakespeare play attending buddy. If you'd told me that would happen on one of our nights out in the 90's I'd have assumed you were high, or crazy, or both.

Things change. People change. Friendships change. Sometimes you find a way to keep the friendship going. Sometimes you accept that right now, the friendship is changing, and perhaps you'll have space for new friends.

When you feel you're leaving people behind:

- Accept that in life, things change, including friendships.

- Be gentle with yourself, allow yourself to be where you are and go where you're going.

- Be gentle with them, allow them to be where they are.

- Trust people with your new self, and look for ways to keep your connection.

- What else? What does your inner wisdom suggest you try?

Dream
Squashing

Dream Squashing

Most of us are absolutely spectacular at squashing our dreams – whether with premature practicality, negativity or perfectionism. We think we're being realistic, sensible, and pragmatic. What we're actually doing is stamping on our dreams before they've had a chance to inspire and lead us. Our dreams come to us for a reason, and if we can keep our practical, logical, left-brain side quiet, those dreams can show us where to go, how to soar, what fun we can have in the following of our dreams.

Squashing your vision with practicality

When I talk to new clients, I find they spend a lot of time squashing their vision with practicality. We start to talk about their vision for their life, and before we've even enjoyed 2 minutes of joyful dreaming, before we've had a chance to connect with the gorgeous "oooh, delicious, I could have that?" feeling of the vision, their Practical side gets involved and beats down the vision with a series of can't do's and impossible's and yes but's.

When you are thinking of your vision, it's the time for your practical side to go and have a cup of tea, to take a break, to chill out and SHUT UP. Don't get me wrong, I'm not trying to demonise the practical side of you – not even slightly. Without that practical side, your dream will remain a dream. But you need the visionary part of you to do the dreaming, while your practical side makes the dream come true.

The inner dreamer's job is to dream, to create, to imagine, to soar with visions of wonder and joy and "ooh, delicious, I could have that?" and "oh man, that would be AWESOME!"

The inner doer's job is to GET SHIT DONE.

But too often, that inner doer gets involved way too early in the dreaming phase, a job it's not good at. So it becomes a Dream Squasher, beating down the dream with practicality. We don't want it to do that.

Give your Inner Doer a new job description: make your vision come to pass.

Imagine it: your Inner Dreamer comes up with a really exciting vision for your life (while your Inner Doer is having a well-deserved rest – feet up with a cup of tea) – a vision that makes your tummy tingle, your feet itch to dance and your body want to jump up and down with joy, excitement and enthusiasm. Then you invite your Inner Doer to come back and make that happen.

The first thing it will probably do (because it's been doing it for so long) is Squash Your Dream with some practical objections. See this as a good thing. If you ignore the Dream Squashing aspect of it, your Inner Doer will have just given you a list of obstacles you need to get over so that you can have your dream. Excellent! Once they're out of the way, following your dream will be a breeze.

Be light and easy and unfazed with this – it's all good, nothing to worry about…just stepping stones to your Big Dream Come True. Once the Inner Doer has laid out all your objections, fears, obstacles and blockages, set it the task of making the vision happen anyway. Get that Inner Doer in its rightful job – the job it was born to do: Carry out the instructions and visions of the Inner Dreamer.

It will take time for your Inner Doer to be retrained though, so be patient. It's like an employee who is used to pen and paper being bamboozled by technology. Just keep reminding it that its job is to do whatever you want to do, no matter what might get in the way. It is worth taking the time to retrain yourself this way. It will make life so much easier.

This practicality that douses the fire of your dreams is often a bit previous. Just keep going after what you want and deal with problems as they arise *if* they arise. Whatever happens, you'll figure it out when it comes up. Whatever happens, you can handle it. You have been all your life, and you're getting better and better at it with time, experience and age. You've got this.

Don't let a dose of premature practicality squash your dreams before they've had a chance to soar. Clear up the objections of your practical side so that you have a clear run to follow your dreams.

When you're squashing your vision with practicality:

- Let your inner dreamer dream – give the inner doer some time off while you're visioning the life you want.

- Remind your inner doer that its job is to make your vision come true, not squash it. (And keep reminding it, for as long as the retraining takes.)

- Use that dream-squashing tendency to find any obstacles in your way.

- Don't forget, whatever comes up, you'll figure it out.

- What else? What does your inner wisdom suggest you try?

Being Realistic

Ugh. Realistic. One of my least favourite words in the world. Because what is "realistic"? Is flight realistic? Electricity? The internet? Brain surgery? Space travel? A black man becoming president in apartheid South Africa? A 17 year old schoolgirl winning a Nobel peace prize after getting shot in the head by the Taliban? A book about a teenage wizard selling 450 million copies? Realism is in the eye of the beholder. It's a concept, not a fact. Many people have done unrealistic things.

And this is why this word annoys me so much – it stops innovation, creativity and dreaming in their tracks, because of a belief, a thought, an opinion. That opinion may or may not be right. It is true that depending on your circumstances, you may find it harder to do something, but it's still possible. Realism, schmealism. So let yourself dream, and dream big. Allow yourself to want what you want.

Who cares if what you want is realistic? It's what you want. Your heart's desires come to you for a reason. Not to torment you with an unrealistic idea that will leave you disappointed and broken, but to tempt you into a new world of possibility and growth. Your visions will take you down paths you never dreamed, where you'll find qualities you didn't know you possessed, and maybe you'll find gold at the end of the rainbow.

Forget whether it's realistic or not – is it possible? Is it doable? Is it conceivable? And are you up for the challenge? Because it may well be a tough, long road, but it's also so much fun. Yes, it's challenging, yes, sometimes it's hard and it hurts and it stretches you and drags you out of your comfort zone. It's also wonderful and exciting and a joyous dance of dream chasing.

And it's true that sometimes that joyous dance can land us on our arse with a bang, when a dose of reality hits. Sometimes it's not a case of build it and they will come, write it and it will sell 400 million copies, or sing and be the next Adele. If your dream is a big one, some of it may well be out of your control.

You do the best you can with what you have and keep taking the action that's yours to take. Take your opportunities, work towards what you want, keep moving forward and see what happens. If other people keep dropping the realism bomb in your lap, maybe it's time to re-consider what you share with them? Dreamers live in a world of possibility and wonder, but not everyone does, so why invite them to upset your apple-cart or freak them out if you don't need to?

I know you want to be able to share your dreams, but don't share them with people who can't cope with them or who have a tendency to stamp on them. Share them with other dreamers, other people who believe in more than they can see, other optimists, other seekers. Just as you don't talk sex with your parents, or football with friends who know nothing about football; share your dreams with those who get it, or are able to support you even when they don't get it.

You can still share with your loved ones even if they're realism-bombers but share in a way that invites them to support you, not bring you down. Tell them what you've done so far, what you'll do next, but not necessarily the world-spanning empire you dream of if you know their minds will be blown by that. Honour yourself, your dreams, and your loved ones tendencies. Once you are starting to take over the world, they'll come round!

When you're being realistic:

- Allow yourself to dream, and dream big. Forget about whether it's realistic. Is it what you want?

- Instead of asking if it's realistic, ask if it's possible.

- Take action - keep doing what you can to make your dreams come true.

- Keep your dreams safe from realism-bombers.

- What else? What does your inner wisdom suggest you try?

Perfectionism, (Too) High Standards and (Too) Big Goals

Now you might think having high standards and big goals is a good thing. After all, shoot for the stars and land on the moon, right? And who wants to work to a low standard? Hell no, but there comes a point when we are slipping into perfectionism, impossibly high standards and goals that are so big, they seem like they're a million miles away. This can be incredibly demotivating, deflating and discouraging.

Don't do it to yourself. Yes, we all dream of getting it perfectly right the first time, of shooting for and landing among the stars with ease, but that is rare. A more common story is striving, trying, improving, falling, failing, learning, aligning, getting close, trying again, doing better next time, expanding, getting it, hitting the moon with delight. Hey, I'm not saying you *can't* do it perfectly right the first time, but just in case you don't, welcome to the 99.99%!

You get to keep growing, learning and getting better day by day. If I had waited until any of my writing was perfect, I wouldn't have released a damn thing yet. As it is, I've written 4 books, have 5 in the works, there are 1000+ blog posts to my name, and I've created courses and cards and journals and podcasts and videos too. None of it is perfect. I released it anyway. By releasing it, I learned to be ok with good enough and I got better with practice.

As perfection is completely impossible, give yourself the chance to improve instead. Moment by moment, word by word, step by step, milestone by milestone. It does get easier. You do learn by doing. At some point, you will be really happy with what you're doing, your reasonable but high expectations will be met and your big goals will be achieved. In the meantime, let yourself learn, grow and get better as you go.

It's also really important to celebrate your progress as well as just completing your big goal. You'll have heard the phrase "the joy is in the journey" and this is so true. For years, I strived, worked hard, put my sights on that finish line, then stumbled over it exhausted and fed up, and I didn't enjoy the achievements that much. If reaching your goal is the only thing that matters, you reach it, have a brief moment of joy, then come up with a new goal…and the stress begins again.

No, no, and a thousand times, NO! Enjoy the journey. Have fun along the way. Celebrate milestones. Look for reasons to celebrate each and every step you take because you will need all of those steps to get to your dream life. One way I do this for my books is to keep a record of the time I spend on a project and the word count. I also throw percentages in there too, because…why not?

This way I get to see milestone numbers to celebrate – every 10 hours, every 10,000 words, every 10% is a reason to celebrate. I get to feel and see that I'm making progress. I also make sure I enjoy the process of writing because if I don't, what's the point?

One of my first coaching clients was a guy with a "5 year plan" who was going to be happy when he got his big goals. I see no sense in that kind of thinking. 5 years of not enjoying life to get a goal we discovered he didn't really want anyway. Ugh. So many people do this - create a happiness postponement until their life is perfect. Don't do that to yourself. Enjoy your life now, on the way to your Big Dreams and goals, not just when all your ducks are in a row. Not least because those pesky ducks will never be in a row.

Life is messy and chaotic, and has plot twists and turns. No matter how hard you try to make everything perfect, to impose impossible expectations, to make it all just so, it won't ever be perfect. Embrace the mess and the chaos and the twists and turns. Embrace the imperfection and the falling short and the road you take to get there (wherever there is for you). Don't get there wishing you'd enjoyed the journey more.

And ultimately, please remember that you are only human. Humans are fallible. They fail, they mess up, they are imperfect, and they have bad days. Maybe you had parents and teachers and employers who expected you to be perfect. They were doing what they thought was right to motivate you to be the best. If that's not working, be human. Be fallible. Allow yourself to be good enough, to get better, to spend every day of your wonderful life learning how to be a better, happier you.

When you are fighting perfectionism, (too) high standards and (too) big goals:

- Let go of the perfectionism, strive for improvement instead.

- Celebrate progress as well as completion, and have fun along the way.

- Don't postpone your happiness until everything is perfect.

- Give yourself a break and accept that you are only human, after all.

- What else? What does your inner wisdom suggest you try?

Negativity, Cynicism and a 'Life's out to get me' attitude

I used to be the most negative, cynical, pessimistic person you could ever hope (not) to meet. I genuinely believed that life was a bitch and then you died.

I got over it.

I believed that optimists were born that way. Some of them perhaps are, but others make themselves into optimists. Simply by choosing a different outlook, day after day after day after day. It took me a good few years to turn myself from cynical and pessimistic to one of the most positive and optimistic people I know. To the point that when a friend was diagnosed with cancer, I was the only one she told because she knew I'd be optimistic about it. Of course I was (and she's fine now, by the way).

How you see things is your choice. You can either see the best, the silver lining, that life is happening *for* you, or you can see the worst, the cloud, that life's happening to you and it's out to get you. I know that when you see things the latter way it doesn't feel like a choice. It feels realistic, like this is real life, this is what it's like – life's shit, against you and everything that happens is designed to pull you down.

It seems like positive people are either naïve and deluded or their life is rosy. Neither are true. Positive people often have to choose over and over and over again to believe that life is good, people are good, there's always a silver lining. A friend of mine grew up in a less than ideal situation, along with her siblings. Two of them are positive people, and two are negative. The positive ones *chose* not to be soured by life.

Everyone has difficulties in their life. We are all touched by illness, by loss, by problems. It's how you choose to see these things, how you choose to respond to life that makes the difference. I promise you that's true, from the heart of a reformed pessimist. I would never have believed it had I not lived it. As an optimist I've faced far worse in life than I did as a cynic, and it's all been easier to deal with because I'm now more positive.

And just in case your defence of your pessimism is that at least you're never disappointed (that used to be my excuse); it is absolute bullshit that pessimists are never disappointed – pessimists live their whole lives disappointed. Since I became an optimist, I am disappointed now and again. When I was a pessimist, every single day of my life was a huge disappointment to me! I know which one I'd prefer to live with.

I know, I know, positive, optimistic people are irritating as hell. But here's the thing: positive people are way less annoying when you are one. The more you hang around with positive people, the more you start to see that they are not *always* positive and sunny, but they'll choose to be positive most of the time. Positivity and optimism are catching, the more time you spend with those positive people, the easier you'll find it to be optimistic and positive.

You don't have to switch instantly from cynic to optimist...just start to look for silver linings, find the bright sides, let your positive friends teach you how to be a little more optimistic. It's way more fun than believing the sky is going to fall in any minute. I know what you're thinking...what if the sky does fall in? You deal with it. Just as you have always dealt with every situation you've found yourself in up to now.

Pessimism doesn't help you deal with bad situations, it actually makes it harder to deal with them. When you're pessimistic, you start from the position of 'this is terrible and there's nothing I can do about it'. How on earth is that helpful? When you're optimistic, you may be knocked on your butt by life, but you're more prepared to jump up and find a way to deal with whatever is thrown at you.

So why not play a different what if game…what if you're wrong that the world is out to get you? What if it *is* possible to have the life you want? What if there are good people out there? What if dreams can come true? What if the world is full of really lovely, helpful people doing good stuff? What if it's all good, always? What if life was happening for you instead of to you? What if you *could* be positive, optimistic and think life's a great adventure?

I know you might have a hard time believing that the world is full of lovely people, especially if you watch and read a lot of news. If aliens arrive on earth and watch the news to find out what the human race is like, they'll think we're all evil, greedy, stupid and corrupt. It's not so. There are many, many more people doing good things in the world. Inventors, geniuses, charitable, kind people doing exciting and interesting and lovely things.

You'd never know about any of them if you just watch or read the news. When I am Queen of the Universe, the media will be forced to report positive, interesting, progressive, kind, good news stories. For now, fear sells papers and gets viewers. Shocking, awful, horrible stories get people tuning in. I shouldn't blame the news outlets for this, they're just working with the world as it is. I do blame them though…but that's another story.

Try a different kind of input – check out things like TED talks, follow people on your social media feeds who are positive and share interesting, good news, and make those feeds a place of good-feeling stuff. I'm always amazed when people tell me their Facebook feed is full of negativity. Mine is a feast of positive, fun stuff – because that's the kind of material I follow, like and comment on. I'm also careful about who's in my *see first* list – mostly inspirational or comedic people and pages. You too can curate what you take in – sensationalist, negative, fear-based news or positive, inspirational, fun stories. It's your choice.

When you're negative, cynical and think life's out to get you:

- Choose a different outlook, one day at a time.
- Seek positive people to talk to, hang out with and be inspired by.
- Play the positive what if game.
- Be mindful about what news and social media you take in.
- What else? What does your inner wisdom suggest you try?

Getting on a negative train of thought

Sometimes you might not be a negative person, but you get on negative trains of thought. Have you ever noticed the destinations of your trains of thought? Are they positive trains that make you feel good about yourself and your life? Or are they negative trains of thought that lead you directly to The Land of I Suck? For example, when you start on the train of thought:

"This chapter isn't flowing" which leads to the thought...

"This is so hard" which leads to the thought...

"Writing is so difficult" which leads to the thought...

"I don't know why I'm trying to do this, I suck" which leads to the thought...

"I'll just go off to Facebook and distract myself from these uncomfortable thoughts" which leads to the thought...

"Oh shit, I've been on Facebook for an hour!" which leads to the thought...

"I suck."

And so on. Do you recognise that kind of train of thought? The train of thought that leads to some version of "I suck"?

I see this so often with clients - they get onto really unhelpful trains of thought, each thought leading them further into The Land Where Everything is Shit and I Suck. Only here's the thing about trains: you can get off at the next stop and get on a different train of thought. Like:

"This chapter isn't flowing."

"Hmm. That's not a train of thought I want to go down."

"I'm only on sentence 3 of the chapter, maybe I can reserve judgement about whether it's flowing or not for another few sentences."

"I love writing."

"I have been really stuck with articles before, and they turned out great."

"In fact, I have some articles I've written about that."

"I could go read them, I could meditate for a minute, or I could go dance around my office for 5 minutes to help unblock the creative pipeline."

"Ha-ha - I wrote an article about that too."

"I'm an extremely prolific writer."

"I rock!"

Now isn't that a better train of thought? It starts in exactly the same place, but ends up at a totally different destination. So if you're prone to getting on unhelpful trains of thought, derail those trains and get on a different train.

One of my favourite techniques to do this is to find a better feeling thought. Simply look for a thought that feels slightly better than the original one (it might not be positive). Keep reaching for something that feels better until you're in the Land of Fun and Positive Thoughts.

For example "I hate my job" -> "My boss is an idiot and makes my life hard" -> "She's not the worst boss I've ever had" -> "It's not the worst job I've ever had" -> "I like some things about it" -> "my colleagues are nice" -> "I've never had so much fun with people as we have here (it's hysteria, mainly, but still)" - > "I've made friends for life here".

Sometimes you'll get to the "I rock" place, sometimes you just get to "it's ok" - as long as it feels better, it's good. The more you do this, the easier it gets. I had a client do this exercise on a particularly persistent train of thought - every time they noticed the starter thought that led to "everything sucks", they stopped and looked for better feeling thoughts.

It wasn't long before they'd totally derailed that habitual negative thought train and replaced it with a positive, fun thought train...which started from the same destination, but ended with "it's all good" or "I need some serious tlc right now", instead of "I suck". [6]

---

[6] Abraham Hicks wrote a whole book about this concept, with examples of using the technique in various scenarios – The Astonishing Power of Emotion, which I highly recommend if you need a bit more help with this idea.

Another way to change trains is to pick a subject you're feeling a bit meh about and find things you love about it. I often get clients to do this about jobs they hate, and despite telling me there is nothing to love, they're usually able to find at least 5 things to love. For example "I love that they pay me", "I love that I met my best mate there", "I love that it's round the corner from my house", "I love the coffee machine", "I love the cleaning lady - she's like a hilarious Yoda". (These are all real examples from clients.)

You can also just pick any subject to have a rampage of love about - your kids, your partner, your pets, the weather. The love train of thought is great fun no matter what you're thinking about. If you're thinking about stuff you love, you're off that negative thought train.

A similar technique is to have a rampage of gratitude. Again, you can do this about the subject you're feeling meh about or just about anything at all in your life. For example, if you're feeling bad about money, do a rampage of gratitude on all the things you have an abundance of (ideas, stationery, books, friends, Netflix shows to watch). The gratitude train of thought is also lots of fun and feels so good.

And most of us have so much to be grateful for, but we forget when we're habitually taking negative thought trains to the Land of Everything Sucks! If you're reading this book, you most likely have an e-reading device, a roof over your head, access to clean and plentiful water, so much stuff that you have a problem with clutter. It's easy to forget how lucky we are. Gratitude rampages will remind you that even if things aren't perfect (no one's life ever is), you still have a lot to appreciate.

Do your best to really feel it – there's no point just listing things you should feel grateful for if you're not feeling it. I get clients to add 'because...' on the end of the "I am grateful" sentence, this deepens the practice and makes you think harder about why you're grateful. For example "I am grateful for the roof over my head because it is keeping me dry today"!

All the above practices are great habits to get into – and you create those great habits the same way you did your negative trains of thought by practicing them over and over and over again.

When you're on a negative train of thought:

- Stop the train and change to a positive one.

- Look for better feeling thoughts.

- Have a rampage of love.

- Have a rampage of gratitude.

- What else? What does your inner wisdom suggest you try?

Negative self-talk and self-criticism

We all have an inner critic or gremlin; or whatever you like to call that nasty voice in your head that is negative and critical and mean and harsh and horrible. It's a magnificent obstacle. Genuinely, it really is – because once you can get this one retrained, it will change your life. Just imagine going through life without that critical commentary in your head.

The first thing to do with this critical inner voice is to make a decision not to treat yourself this way. You wouldn't speak to anyone else that way (not if you expected them to speak to you again), so don't talk to yourself like that. By the way, *don't demonise* the inner critic or gremlin or ego. They're still a part of you, an important part of you and demonising any part of you doesn't help you become whole and fabulous.

Instead, look at understanding that part of you. Every part of every body has a positive intention – and the inner critic's intention is usually to get the best from you. The trouble is that most of us aren't overly inspired and motivated by criticism – it actually has the exact opposite effect on many of us, making us doubt ourselves, feel bad about ourselves and fearful of trying anything new.

As we grew up, we probably saw a lot of self-criticism as a motivator – perhaps you had a teacher who did that, or you saw a parent criticise themselves? But it doesn't work. It's time to introduce a new way of working, even if you have been criticising yourself for the past 10/20/30/70 years. Let's update the old software. Look at what the positive intention is of that negative self-talk, and find a new way to achieve the same end.

When I explored my inner critic's motives, I found she wanted to help me be the best I can be. She was actually quite cross that

I wasn't appreciative. I gave her a new way to help me be the best I can be: encouragement. Use that skill of laser-sharp focus on your faults to point out your strengths, what you are great at, what you're doing well, how you're awesome. It's a small tweak to use the skills of the inner critic for good, not evil.

Of course it takes time, and anyone who's been doing a job one way for decades needs an adjustment period to get used to a new way of working. Be very gentle with yourself in this transition; criticising yourself for criticising yourself is not only the height of irony, it's completely counter-productive.

Your inner critic may also be more active when you're tired or unwell – again, this is a good thing. She's pointing something out to you; she's a great custodian of your self-care. So pay attention and make sure you are taking care of yourself, loving yourself, being good to yourself. When you do this, you may find your inner critic pipes down because you're feeling loved.

To help the transition from self-criticism to self-love, look for words you'd like to hear about yourself – affirmations about how fabulous you are. You're learning a new language, so find some new words to practice. Affirmations can be a great way to retrain yourself not to negative self-talk – as soon as you notice you're criticising yourself (and you will, until you don't), you can bust out your favourite affirmation and switch the energy around entirely. Here's a few of my favourites:

- ✓ I deeply and completely love and accept myself…always
- ✓ I trust myself; I'm always doing the best I can
- ✓ I dance through life with joy and ease
- ✓ I am a magnet for good stuff
- ✓ Every day, every year, life gets better and better

In any and every way you can, train yourself to see what's good about you, how you're doing well, what you're good at. Turn that negative self-talk around to positive self-talk, start feeling good about yourself and taking excellent care of yourself. Negative self-talk is simply a habit you've got into, and habits can be changed.

When your self-talk is negative:

- Make the decision not to talk to yourself like that.

- Find the positive intention behind the negative self-talk and retrain yourself to do that another (nicer) way.

- Be gentle with yourself while you retrain your inner critic to be nice – there's no point trying to retrain the inner critic by being critical.

- Replace those critical statements with positive, encouraging, empowering statements.

- What else? What does your inner wisdom suggest you try?

"I don't want my dream anymore"

This one is not exactly an obstacle, it is more a potential exit route on your dream journey. Sometimes as we grow and change, we find that our old dreams have changed – there is nothing wrong with this, you're allowed to change your mind. On the other hand, beware. Fear can put on "I don't want this anymore" clothes and disguise itself to stop you when you genuinely do want something.

So, how do you tell which it is? You may have a sense already, simply by thinking about fear versus a genuine change of mind – trust yourself if that is the case. One thing to check is how you're feeling. If you're feeling tired, not feeling cared for and you're not enjoying life, this can skew the results in fear's favour.

I've wanted to give up on my business at least twice a year for more than a decade. Every time I wanted to give up, I was tired, uncared-for and not having any fun. Once I felt better, the problem went away all by itself. Check your self-care, self-love, energy and joy. When you feel better, come back and ask yourself if you want the same vision, or if what you want has changed.

I've also come up against this obstacle when my vision for my life and business has changed. I don't want what I wanted five years ago, or even two years ago for that matter. It wasn't that I didn't want any of it, it had just changed and evolved. Sometimes all you need to do is make a small tweak to your vision and your enthusiasm will come flooding back.

Often as we grow into our dreams, they expand. Our dreams don't want to scare us away in the early days, so they'll just give a little bit of the picture. For example, maybe leaving the *20 million selling author* bit until after you've got used to the idea of writing one book. So check if your dream is bigger than it was, or if it has changed direction.

One of my clients had a dream of having the freedom to be location independent, being able to work from anywhere in the world. As she was working towards that dream, she met a guy and started a family. When she came to me, she was conflicted...she was loving being home with her family but what about her dream? Her dream had changed to having the freedom to spend time with her family, and travel with them. It hadn't gone away, it had just changed.

You have within you all the guidance you need to check in on this obstacle – your body and heart will tell you. Take a moment to relax your body, then think about giving up on your vision – how is your body reacting? Your thoughts may try to jump in and say "Yeah, but..." - ignore them, just notice your body's reaction. Does it tense up or relax? Do you feel excitement or anxiety? What message does your body want to tell you about your dream?

Next, take 3 deep breaths into your heart and ask your heart what you need to do. Once again, your thoughts may try to leap in, but let your heart answer. Your heart may leap or sink, it may feel happy or sad, there may be heartache or joy, there may be a feeling that the desire is gone or a feeling you want to keep fighting. Just notice what your heart has to say about your dreams.

Even when your thoughts are going through the pros and cons and trying to convince you of one course of action or another, your body and heart know what is real for you and will give you true answers, not fearful or sensible, logical ones you think sound right or make sense. The heart wants what it wants, and sometimes that doesn't look linear or right or fit your five year plan, but it's what's true for you, so trust it.

It is hard to let go of a dream you've wanted for years, but if it's the right thing for you, then let it go. This is the only way you can go after what you really truly want. While you're holding on to old dreams you no longer feel passionate about, new dreams are waiting on the sidelines for you to notice them. It is rare I will say to someone to let go of their dream, but if you don't want it anymore, it's a dream that's already let go of you.

Just make sure you are not giving up on your dream because it got a bit tough. If you really want it, keep trying to make it happen. Dreams do sometimes get tough. We feel like they should be easy-breezy, floaty-dancing-in-the-meadow journeys, but often they are challenging and difficult and look utterly impossible. If you still want it, work on your resilience, your tenacity and your confidence. And if you don't, go dance to the tune of a new dream.

When you don't want your dream anymore:

- Check on your self-care, self-love, energy and joy.

- Has your vision changed? Sometimes a tiny tweak is all you need to get you back on track.

- Go to the wisdom of your body and heart and ask them what is going on.

- If you truly don't want your old dream anymore, let it go and move onto something you *do* want.

- What else? What does your inner wisdom suggest you try?

Procrastination

Procrastination

I decided procrastination deserved its own section, because so many of us blame procrastination for the lack of progress on our dreams. We just put things off all the time for no apparent good reason…only that's not strictly true. There are usually many factors behind the procrastination.

Procrastination is the symptom, not the disease.

It's like just throwing pills at the symptom of insomnia…it might work in the short term, but if you don't sort out the reasons for the insomnia, you'll be dependent on pills forever.

And hey, if saying "I'm procrastinating" worked, I'd say go with it, keep on kicking your own butt, but it doesn't. It actively HURTS. People label themselves procrastinators and it doesn't help them get whatever they want to do done. It doesn't help them feel great about themselves (in fact, it's often the direct opposite). In fact, I'll go as far as to say that labelling it procrastination actually gets in the way of getting the task done.

Because you're procrastinating, so you *should* just do it, right? But you're not. Because you're procrastinating. And there's nothing you can do about you procrastinating. Other than force yourself to do it…and if you could do that, you wouldn't be procrastinating. A beautifully circular argument that there's no way out of. What if instead you said to yourself "hey, I'm putting X off, what's going on?" and fixed the underlying problem so you can crack on with your task?!

I know, sometimes you are just procrastinating, and giving yourself a swift kick up the backside works (it doesn't make you a bad person) but most of the time, a slight change of focus will help far more than beating yourself up for procrastinating. Over the years, I've developed a series of questions to ask yourself about whatever you're putting off.

These are the questions I've been asking clients about procrastination since 2010. The problem is almost always one of these underlying causes, not that they are just lazy, bad people who need a good kick up the jacksie. It's been far more helpful for my clients (and me) to identify the true issue, not just say we procrastinate. I sincerely hope it will help you too.

Question 1: Do you want to do it?

I always have to start with this one because it's the biggie. If you don't want to do it, of course you will put it off and put it off and put it off! So if it's not something you actually want to do, check first if it's something that really has to be done. Do you have to go to the gym? No? So forget about it. Find another way to get fit. Do you have to do your accounts? Yes. Could someone else do them? If so, why not get some help? I know you are superwoman and you can do everything yourself, but the joy of living in the 21st century is that you don't have to. If you genuinely *have to* do it and you can't get help, you've just got to do it, find a way to make it fun so you can get it done.

I get it. For years, I put off doing my accounts – they're boring, tedious, and dull, dull, dull. Then a few years ago, I put on my favourite music, turned it up loud and cracked on. That made it better. The following year, I added a timer and did an hour at a time. That also made it better because it was only an hour, and I was playing good music and dancing at the same time. Now, I aim to do 10-20 minutes every week to keep on top of it, so I don't have to do hours at a time. This helps me get this tedious task done. A whole lot faster than when I tried to do it all in one go and put if off for months on end.

If you don't want to do it: don't do it, delegate it or make it fun.

Question 2: Are you ready to do it?

If you're not ready, this is not procrastination…it's not being ready. I had a client who was procrastinating a piece of homework I had set. When we were investigating why, he said he didn't have a notepad to do it in. It wasn't the homework that was the problem, it was the lack of the right equipment. As soon as he got the notepad, he did the homework. It's amazing how often small things like this get in the way, and while you're busy blaming yourself for procrastination, you're missing that you need something to get ready to do the task.

Whenever I've done website updates, I've procrastinated for months, because I'm ruminating, I'm mulling, I'm pondering what exactly I want to say. I'm not procrastinating, I'm just not ready to take action. This procrastination saves me hours of wasted work – if I'd just made myself get on with it, I'd have had to change the website again two months later when I'd decided what I really wanted to say.

If you're not ready, get ready.

Question 3: Is there a better way to do it?

I had a client who had some sales calls to make, and he was procrastinating. I ran him through this checklist: do you want to do it? Yes. Are you ready? Yes. Is there a better way? Yes! It turned out that 3 of the 50 people on his list hated to be sold to by phone. So for them, the better way was to set up a face to face meeting.

Here's what cracks me up though: he was so busy beating himself up for procrastinating, he had put off all 50 calls because of 3 that needed to be done differently. As soon as we identified that better way for those 3, he made the other calls. It can be that simple when you recognise that procrastination itself is just the symptom of a deeper issue and you look for that issue.

If there's a better way, do it that way.

Question 4: Do you know what to do?

Again, this makes me laugh, because if you don't know exactly what to do, how do you expect to do it? I have had this conversation a lot with clients who are working on websites. They're procrastinating. Only they're not procrastinating, they just have no idea what to do. The answer to this one is super-easy – you just find out what to do next.

Make it easy for yourself and find a baby step – a next step that can be taken in about 10 minutes. It's hard to procrastinate teeny tiny baby steps, because they're clear and easy. Your baby step might be to ask a friend or google it, sit and brainstorm for 10 minutes, or pick one thing off your brainstorm list and do that.

Also, not knowing what to do can be a case of not having *defined* exactly what you're going to do. I procrastinate a lot at my desk when I haven't picked a task to do next. So it's not exactly procrastination, it's that I haven't chosen what to do. Once I do, I then get it done (or procrastinate for a different reason).

If you don't know what to do, you're not procrastinating, you just need to figure out specifically what to do.

Question 5: Are you trying to do step 98 before step 1?

On big, ambitious projects we can easily get ahead of ourselves. For example, worrying about sending a proposal to the publisher before we've actually figured out what we want to write about. It's a beautiful way of tying bricks to your feet and ensuring you can't move. It's not that helpful in getting shit done though. Once again, the good old baby step comes to the rescue here.

Itty bitty, teeny weeny baby steps make life so much easier…and when you start to break it down you'll notice that before you can put the head-shots on your website you need: 1. To get said head-shots done, 2. To get jpegs of them, 3. To find out how to upload them. No wonder you're procrastinating "putting head-shots on your website"…there's a load of stuff that needs to happen first. (This is a real example from a client that made me laugh out loud when we figured out *why* it was being procrastinated on.)

If you're trying to do step 98 before step 1, break it down, figure out the next teeny tiny baby step, and do that.

Question 6: Do you know you CAN do it?

Lack of confidence isn't procrastination, it's lack of confidence. If you aren't convinced you can do something, of course you're going to put it off because no one likes to fail. No one wants to set themselves up to make a total arse of themselves. If you're unconfident in your ability or feel a task is impossible, you'll put it off. It's human nature. It doesn't make you a bad person, it makes you normal.

I've done it, everyone I've ever worked with has done it and everyone I know has done it. So, what do you need to do? Increase your confidence, build yourself up, get inspired. Most things we want to do aren't impossible, and most have been done by normal people just like you. Give yourself a big pep talk, go find other people who've done it and get inspired, put your cheerleaders on the case or work on your skills so you KNOW you can do it. (By the way, I'm not talking about taking years to do this, I'm talking about taking action now so you can do it real soon.)

Once again, you can use the power of the baby step here – you may not believe you can do the whole big task, but maybe you could just do the next action? And the next. Before long, you'll have done the thing you weren't sure you could do – one baby step at a time.

If you're not sure you can do it: build yourself up, get support, get inspired, take baby steps and do it despite not being sure you can.

Question 7: Is the timing right to do it?

I deliberately left this one until last, because it's more often one of the other factors; but sometimes there is an element of Divine Timing. Sometimes things just come together at a certain time, and you find yourself doing something you've been putting off for a while. Like the book I'll be working on next – I first had the idea in 2007 and created a mini ebook, which I always knew would expand into a full book one day.

In the last couple of years, a few more pieces have fallen into place, rounding out the ideas in the book and making it a more complete self-care guide. For years, I've wondered why I've been procrastinating on that book. Only I wasn't, I was waiting for the final pieces to come to me. In 2018, that will be my Major Project and the book will finally be written – a decade after the idea first came to me. It will also be a lot better than it would have been if I'd written it earlier.

If the timing's not right, relax…you'll do it when the timing is right.

If you've got this far and none of these questions uncovered the reason you've been procrastinating, here's one more question to ask yourself to figure out what is going on...

Question 8: What's stopping you doing this task?

Because I know that you are a brilliant, intuitive, remarkable human, and I also know that procrastination is a symptom, not a cause. So, let's find the real cause, and you know yourself best, so you know what's getting in your way. Fix that, and your procrastination will be cured. Occasionally the answer will be nothing. So if that's the case you can get on and do it, but more often there is something in the way – find that, and procrastination will not be a problem for you.

Do you have an obstacle I missed?

So, there you have it – these are all the obstacles I could think of when I was writing this book – many that I have bumped up against myself and that my clients over the past decade or more have shared. It's not a comprehensive list of every obstacle you could ever come up against, but I hope it has given you some ideas on how to get over, under, round or through anything that may block your path.

I'd love to hear your experience with this book. Did you find obstacles that were in your way? Has the book helped you moved past some obstacles? Is there something I missed? Are you still stuck? What did your inner wisdom suggest you do? Let me know via donnaonthebeach.com, facebook.com/donnaonthebeach or Twitter - @donnaonthebeach - how you're getting on and if I can help at all. I love helping people bust past their obstacles.

If you enjoyed this book...

Fall in Love With Life

By Donna Higton

Get book one in the "Foundations of Life" series FREE today.

This is your one and only life... are you loving it?

Or are you wondering where your mojo went?

It's time to fall in love with life

Get the book free here:

www.donnaonthebeach.com/blog/loveyourlife

This is your one and only life - are you fully, deeply, completely head over heels in love with it, or are you wondering what happened to your dreams, your joy and your mojo? No matter what's happening in your life, you can start to fall in love with it right now, even if it's not perfect, even if you want to change everything about it, you can still dance joyfully through life.

In this book, Donna shares her favourite techniques, tips and tools for helping you fall deeply, madly in love with your life right now. Drawn from her own experience of falling in love with life, and coaching clients all over the world since 2004, this book is a celebration of joy, laughter and happy dances.

Praise for "Fall in Love With Life"

"I love this book for many reasons... but mostly because it doesn't feel in any way that you're being force fed a formula for happiness. It's genuine, funny and irreverent at the same time that it feels sacred. Donna's tongue in cheek way of guiding comes through on every page and honestly, reading this book alone is a brilliant way to fall in love with life...

- Stacy Nelson, Author of Writing the Damn Book

"It's the kind of book that puts me in a good mood, that's for sure. Some of the ideas I think I'll be trying first include 'taking excellent care of myself' along with embracing my inner geek (if you love it, who cares whether it's fashionable?) and taking dance breaks. With the curtains shut. I'm giving this delightful, cheerful and inspiring read a positively loved-up five bites."

- Sarah Clark, Author of "Gorgeously Full Fat", blogger and bookeaters reviewer

Note from the Author

I truly hope you enjoyed this book, and that you have busted some obstacles! If you feel inclined to leave a review on your favourite book review platform, I would really appreciate it.

This is book 3 of the "Dreams Come True" series…I haven't written books one and two yet (it's a long story!) but if you'd like to be the first to read the others in the series, come on over to donnaonthebeach.com and join my list – my weekly e-mail readers are always among the first to hear about new projects and releases.

This book has been through many edits, with several people, and even several software programs, but nothing is infallible and you might have caught an error or spelling mistake…if you did, I'd be very grateful if you'd let me know. Spelling and grammar mistakes make me twitch and yet, some always seem to slip through the net, so if you spot one, come to donnaonthebeach.com to let me know, or you can find me under 'Donnaonthebeach' on Facebook and Twitter.

(Please note, I'm British, so if you're elsewhere in the world, you may spell things a little differently to me.)

Thank you, may you fall head over heels in love with your life, make your deepest dreams come true and bust through every obstacle life puts in your way!

About Donna

I work with women (and a few men) who *know* there is more to life; I help them to fall in love with their lives, connect to their guidance, find their deepest dreams and make them a reality. My deepest dream is to be laid-back, loving life, joyfully creating difference-making, inspired work (and to spend more time by the sea than I get to now). You will find me in the centre of England surrounded by paper, pens, books, Kindles and probably chocolate.

Come on over to www.donnaonthebeach.com to find more articles, products, and fabulous freebies to help you make the most of your wonderful life.

Connect with me at:
www.donnaonthebeach.com
www.facebook.com/donnonathebeach
@donnaonthebeach on Twitter and Instagram

"The First Step to a Joyful Life"

I've been teaching clients the benefits of creating super strong self-care foundations since 2007 – it's the cornerstone of my coaching program.

In this ebook, you will learn:

Why self-care is so important (and what it has to do with axes!)

The 7 top excuses we use to NOT take care of ourselves…and how to bust past them

How to listen to the messages of your body, mind, heart and soul

101 self-care ideas (you don't have to do them all!)

How to create an easy and fun self-care plan that you can start today, no matter how busy and important you are

– Available free at
http://www.donnaonthebeach.com/blog/firststep

Upcoming Titles

Make sure you're on my mailing list to be informed of future titles (there's another 9 books in the pipeline right now!): www.donnaonthebeach.com/blog/freebies

CPSIA information can be obtained
at www.ICGtesting.com
Printed in the USA
LVHW031408310320
651774LV00028B/1101